THE **21** *DAY*

CRUCIFIXION

CHALLENGE

M. J. Welcome

Other Books by M. J. Welcome:

Overcome Secret Sins in 15 Days

Battling for the Light

© 2016 Michelle J. Dyett-Welcome. All rights reserved.

No Part of this book may be reproduced, stored in retrieval system, or transmitted by any means without the written permission of the author.

SMART PUBLISHING HOUSE
A Division of MDW Consulting Group
Far Rockaway, New York
www.smartpublishinghouse.com

Editing | Layout S.M.A.R.T Copy Designs
Proofreaders | Mary Ball | Matteel Welcome
S.M.A.R.T Copy Designs
www.smartcopydesignsinc.com

First Published by Smart House Publishing
06/02/16

Library of Congress Control Number: 2016911601
ISBN-13: 978-0692731475
ISBN-10: 0692731474

Printed in the U.S.A.

Surrendering

My *all*

To Jesus.

Table of Contents

APPRECIATION |vi

INTRODUCTION |vii

THE PATH OF CRUCIFICTION |xii

CHALLENGE DAY 1 |xvi

CHALLENGE DAY 2 |23

CHALLENGE DAY 3 |33

CHALLENGE DAY 4 |41

CHALLENGE DAY 5 |49

CHALLENGE DAY 6 |61

CHALLENGE DAY 7 |71

CHALLENGE DAY 8 |85

CHALLENGE DAY 9 |97

CHALLENGE DAY 10 |109

CHALLENGE DAY 11 |121

CHALLENGE DAY 12	130
CHALLENGE DAY 13	141
CHALLENGE DAY 14	149
CHALLENGE DAY 15	155
CHALLENGE DAY 16	167
CHALLENGE DAY 18	181
CHALLENGE DAY 19	193
CHALLENGE DAY 20	201
CHALLENGE DAY 21	209
CONCLUSION	220

APPRECIATION

Father, I thank you for your goodness toward me. I thank you for laying this challenge on my heart and for giving me the strength to complete it.

Special thanks to the members of the His Facebook Prayer Group who faithfully completed the original 21 day Challenge.

To my friend Mary L. Ball who helped proofread this book. I want you to know that I appreciate you! My life is richer and more blessed since you have come into it.

Dwain, thank you for all your support and encouragement. You are my husband, but you are also my encourager and my best friend. May the Lord continue to bless you.

INTRODUCTION

On the morning of May 3, 2016, the Lord showed me something unusual. It was a challenge.

Often in life, we challenge ourselves in many areas such as sports, work, New Year's resolutions, in our health, our habits, and even our attitudes. However, on that day the Lord issued a challenge that would help improve our spiritual selves if we opted to press in for *21 days*.

The challenge was not for everyone.
- It is for those who were willing to commit.
- Those who desire to be more through the power and leading of God.

- Those who are longing to go to a higher level.
- Moreover, it is for those who were determined to become mature through reason of use.

"But strong meat belongeth to them that are of full age, even those who by reason of use have their senses exercised to discern both good and evil."
⚜ Hebrews 5:14

"And if one prevail against him, two shall withstand him; and a threefold cord is not quickly broken."
⚜ Ecclesiastes 4:12

From the above verse, we also see that the number 3 possesses *strength*, which is **not easily or quickly broken**. A force that is able to withstand assault.

According to E. W. Bullinger, the number 3 is significant because it denotes something that is complete, real, solid and substantial. It symbolizes divine perfection.

The number 3:
http://www.biblebelievers.org.au/number07.htm

Why is this important? May is the fifth month of the year and it oozes with grace. It signifies a month of favor. The kind of favor that God shows to the unworthy, to those that suffer, to the stubborn, and to those who are miserable. God's favor comes in the form of mercy, compassion, patience, and grace.

The number 5:
http://www.biblebelievers.org.au/number09.htm

When we put this together, we see that God's notification of a challenge was *rigged* for our success! Therefore, the anointing of favor was upon it. God will favor us with strength and divine perfection so that we can become who we are meant to be in Jesus name.

When does the challenge officially begin? As soon, as you consent and agree to start.

God will do a new and creative work in you. He will cause the former things to pass away as he ushers in a new thing in your life. In this sense, you will experience the reality of the number 4, which represents creation.

The number 4: http://www.biblebelievers.org.au/number08.htm

Together we will embark on a spiritual challenge with the Lord. The challenge will begin with the first chapter in the book of Jeremiah beginning at verse 4.

The objective is to create a new path that is deeper in the Lord. To gain strength to grow in understanding and wisdom. To discover whom we are meant to be and to realize what God intends for us to accomplish.

In order to realize our spiritual potential and live our divine mandate we need to recognize what excuses or hindrances are holding us back.

Are you ready to get started?

May the Lord grant you success as you embark on this challenge. May he open your eyes and expand your understanding. May you grow in wisdom to the glory of God.

M.J. Welcome

THE PATH OF CRUCIFICTION

"And he said to them all, If any man will come after me, let him deny himself, and take up his cross daily, and follow me."
✢ Luke 9:23

Luke 9:23, sums up the reality of a believer's life in Christ Jesus. It is a life of denial. It is one full of pain, sacrifice, and trials. The word denial is to affirm that we do not have a connection or acquaintance with anyone. It is to forget ourselves, to lose sight of our own interests in order to take up our cross and follow Jesus.

It is a life full of separation from what we have known, who we were, and the things that we formally enjoyed. It is a *departing*. It speaks of distance being placed between something and us. It could be the distance of time or place.

Based on the root meaning of **deny** (*arneomai*) we are called to act totally unlike our former selves. We are to prove our former selves *false*. We are to pour forth, utter, or to speak this fact. "I am a new creature for my old nature is nailed to the cross."

"Therefore if any man [be] in Christ, [he is] a new creature: old things are passed away; behold, all things are become new."
⚜ 2 Corinthians 5:17

Oswald Chambers states it is, "signing the death warrant of the disposition of sin in us." It is the recognition that we are the ones who should have been hung on the cross. As we progress along the crucifixion path, we realize that although we live, it is Christ who lives in us. Our human body remains, but the old "Satanic right to myself is gone."

The Apostle Paul stated it this way . . .

"For that which I do I allow not: for what I would, that do I not; but what I hate, that do I. If then I do that which I would not, I consent unto the law that it is good. Now then it is no more I that do it, but sin that dwelleth in me. For I know that in me (that is, in my flesh,) dwelleth no good thing: for to will is present with me; but how to perform that which is good I find not. For the good that I would I do not: but the evil which I would not, that I do. Now if I do that I would not, it is no more I that do it, but sin that dwelleth in me. I find then a law, that, when I would do good, evil is present with me. For I delight in the law of God after the inward man:"
⚜ Romans 17:16-22

He called out what was false and established what was true.

"It is the spirit that quickeneth; the flesh profiteth nothing: the words that I speak unto you, they are spirit, and they are life."
⚜ *John 6:63*

In order to live in Christ Jesus, we have to be willing to die. When we are dead to our former lusts, affections, desires and interests that is when we are truly alive in Christ Jesus.

"I am crucified with Christ: nevertheless I live; yet not I, but Christ liveth in me: and the life which I now live in the flesh I live by the faith of the Son of God, who loved me, and gave himself for me."
⚜ *Galatians 2:20*

There is no escaping the reality of a believer's life. It is one full of death and the pains of crucifixion.

"And they that are Christ's have crucified the flesh with the affections and lusts."
⚜ *Galatians 5:24*

Christ makes it very clear that there is no other way for us to live the abundant life.

"Verily, verily, I say unto you, Except a corn of wheat fall into the ground and die, it abideth alone: but if it die, it bringeth forth much fruit."
⚜ John 12:24

We must die. We must pick up our cross. If we do not we are "not worthy" of him.

"And he that taketh not his cross, and followeth after me, is not worthy of me."
⚜ Matthew 10:38

Are you ready to DIE?

CHALLENGE

DAY 1

GOD

FORMED US

PRAYER

Father, in the name of Jesus we bless you because you have granted unto us life and favor in this new season. We ask that you establish us in your ways, in truth, and maturity. Let the meditations of our hearts be acceptable in your sight. Let it bring you glory and establish us as monuments for your glory, in Jesus name we pray, amen.

THE 21 DAY

SCRIPTURAL FOCUS

"Then the word of the LORD came unto me, saying, Before I formed thee in the belly I knew thee; and before thou camest forth out of the womb I sanctified thee, and I ordained thee a prophet unto the nations."

✟ Jeremiah 1:4-5

Many of you may have already read the full chapter of Jeremiah and your tenacious attitude must be commended! It shows your determination to get what God has for you in this season. It is my earnest hope and prayer that you get it with substantial increase, in Jesus name.

Some of you may not have had a chance to do so, but I pray that you will do so soon. The fact that you showed up here is also worth noting. I thank the Lord that you have desired in your heart to *grow* more in the Lord. May the Lord establish your roots and help you to flourish as you pursue him, in Jesus name.

CRUCIFIXION CHALLENGE

LESSON

In Jeremiah 1:4-5, we see that the Word of the Lord came to the prophet and that word was *information*. It was knowledge. God disclosed to him what the prophet had not known before. Maybe he suspected. Perhaps he wondered. However, God established the fact that he formed Jeremiah in the belly, he knew Jeremiah before he came out of the womb. He sanctified him and ordained him for a *purpose*.

Yatsar is the Hebrew word for formed. It means to frame or fashion something. It denotes divine activity; it is an act of creation (Genesis 2:7-8). It is to be pre-ordained. Its root meaning is to be narrow, cramped, besieged or be in a strait. It is to be distressed (Genesis 32:7 and 1 Samuel 30:6). However, it also means to spread out, to lay or to make a bed (Psalm 139:8).

THE 21 DAY

Yatsar shows us the duality of Jeremiah's calling. He was to walk in the narrow ways of God, which would often result in distress, yet he was to spread out in confidence knowing that wherever he was and whatever he faced God was with him.

MEDITATION

Meditate on the word *yatsar*. What do you hear? How has God formed you? What are you to be? How are you to operate?

What has Holy Spirit placed on your heart to ask God in order for the formation of God to manifest in your life?

CRUCIFIXION CHALLENGE

THE 4 MINUTE CHALLENGE

For 4 minutes, pray to the Lord in the spirit. Give him permission to create something new in you. If you are not able to pray in Holy Ghost (tongues), then allow Holy Spirit to prompt you as to what you should pray. If nothing comes to mind do not despair, it just means that you will have to press harder and be more determined to breakthrough!

Put on some praise music and begin to sing and exalt the Lord. If you are not in a place where you can praise God, grab your Bible. Ask Holy Spirit to identify for you what scripture you should read. You can also open your Bible to a random page trusting God to lead you to the chapter or verse that will meet your need.

PRAYER

Father, we thank you for this opportunity to learn how you have fashioned us. Fulfill your purpose in our lives; cause us to realize our pre-ordained destiny through Christ Jesus.

THE 21 DAY

Conform us to the image of Jesus. Let your beauty come forth through every test, distress, tribulation, or suffering in the name of Jesus. Forge and refine us so that we will come out as pure as gold we pray, amen.

"For whom he did foreknow, he also did predestinate to be conformed to the image of his Son, that he might be the firstborn among many brethren."
⚜ Romans 8:29

CHALLENGE

DAY 2

DESIRE

TO BE KNOWN

PRAYER

Father, as we embark on day two of our spiritual challenge we ask that you go before us and prepare the way. We ask that you open our eyes, hearts, and minds in the name of Jesus. We ask that you give us the perception of hearing so that we will grow in spiritual discernment in Jesus name.

THE 21 DAY

Father, we ask that you cover our sins and throw them into the sea of forgetfulness (Micah 7:19). Let them not speak out against us. Thank you for hearing and answering us this day, amen.

SCRIPTURAL FOCUS

"Then the word of the LORD came unto me, saying, Before I formed thee in the belly I knew thee; and before thou camest forth out of the womb I sanctified thee, and I ordained thee a prophet unto the nations."

⚜ Jeremiah 1:4-5

Yesterday we learned about how God formed Jeremiah, how he knew him, and how he set him apart as holy unto himself. God is not a respecter of persons therefore, as he has formed, knew, and set Jeremiah apart, so has he done for each of us as well.

"For there is no respect of persons with God."

⚜ Romans 2:11

CRUCIFIXION CHALLENGE

This fact should cause us to feel great gratitude and tremendous joy! For while we were in our mother's belly God prepared us for all that we would face in life. He made us with the ability to withstand distress and the capacity to thrive in adverse conditions.

LESSON

Today we will go beyond the surface and find out what it means to be known by God. The Hebrew word *yada'* is used to convey the enormity of what it means to be known. It means to be knowledgeable about, to perceive, to have awareness gained by experience, to be distinguished, or to discriminate, and to be revealed.

In every way possible, God knows us. There is nothing hidden from the Lord. He knows all our dirty secrets, our habits, generational sins, the curses that plague us, and the things we fear others may find out. In spite of this, he loves us! Before we sin, God knows. Before we fall, he is aware. Before we deny him through doubt, fear, or worry it is known as it was with Peter. So why is it hard for us to live out in the open? Why is it that we try to hide behind fig leaves or lurk in the shadows of obscurity?

If God knows, why should it matter if mere men know? This should be a freeing thought. Yet for many it may fill them with tremendous fear. God told Jeremiah that before he was formed in the belly of his mother that He knew him.

What happens in the belly of a woman? The child is shaped in the ways of iniquity. Generational sins are passed down. Generational curses stake their claim over the lives of the unborn child.

"Behold, I was shapen in iniquity; and in sin did my mother conceive me."
⚜ Psalm 51:5

CRUCIFIXION CHALLENGE

Yet there is also another reality. A reality that is rooted in pure truth. Before we were formed, God knew us and designed a purpose for us based on his knowledge of who we were to become in him.

"For whom he did foreknow, he also did predestinate to be conformed to the image of his Son, that he might be the firstborn among many brethren."
⚜ Romans 8:29

Many are called to the great purpose, of becoming sons of God, but few will be chosen in the end.

"For many are called, but few are chosen."
⚜ Matthew 22:14

THE 21 DAY

How can you make sure you are chosen? You must consent and agree to the process of God. You must be willing to allow him to form you. You must believe that he knows everything about you including the things that the enemy will try to exploit in order to sift you, shake you, or break you in pieces.

MEDITATION

Are there areas in your life that you have locked God out of? Are there things about yourself that you have tried to hide from God? Are you afraid for others to know your weaknesses, faults, or shortcomings?

God knows them. He has made provisions for them. There is no need to be fearful of making them known to mere men.

"Confess your faults one to another, and pray one for another, that ye may be healed. The effectual fervent prayer of a righteous man availeth much."
⚜ James 5:16

CRUCIFIXION CHALLENGE

If you are terrified of letting others know that you have sinned or that you need help, the danger is not what they will think of you. The real issue is that Satan is within your boarders. For the word of the Lord says if we confess our faults to one another then healing will be ours. If we exercise wisdom and follow the unction and direction of Holy Spirit, we will avail much.

Fear of what others will think of us, how they will view us, or how they will treat us is an obstacle to healing. The enemy will whip out his trump card of *fear* to stop us dead in our tracks.

The 5 MINUTE CHALLENGE

Today, take time to pray in the spirit for 5 minutes. Ask God to identify any area where you are fearful. Areas where you are worried about what others will think of you if they knew. Are there things you have tried to hide? Lay hold of your freedom today.

THE 21 DAY

God has not given you a spirit of fear. In fact, he has defused it because he has made it known to you that he knew you before you were formed. He knows everything that has gone into making you the person that you are and he still loves you. He still died for you. This fact establishes your *value* to him. Saving you was worth the price that was paid. Honor him by shedding all fear, worry, and anxiety over what men think of you.

PRAYER

Glory be to God who has freed us through the work of Jesus. Thank you for knowledge so that we would not perish. Father keep this understanding fresh in our minds. Help us to walk with knowledge and to live it out daily.

Father, we ask that everything the enemy has built in us be torn down in the name of Jesus. Make the walls fall like the walls of Jericho. Father, please build us a new. Cause us to be beautiful, fortified monuments unto the Lord.

CRUCIFIXION CHALLENGE

We bless you for such a wonderful and glorious calling. May all be manifest to the honor of your name, and to the crowning glory of Jesus we pray, amen.

CHALLENGE
DAY 3

CALLED

TO HOLINESS

PRAYER

Glory to God the One who has called us! We bless you for you have created for us a hope and a future. Father, help us as we continue with your spiritual challenge. Help us to grow, mature, and be enlightened. Open our understanding. Help us to increase in the knowledge of Christ Jesus. May we become brighter lights in a darkened world, amen.

THE 21 DAY

SCRIPTURAL FOCUS

"Then the word of the LORD came unto me, saying, Before I formed thee in the belly I knew thee; and before thou camest forth out of the womb I sanctified thee, and I ordained thee a prophet unto the nations."

⚜ Jeremiah 1:4-5

Yesterday we learned what it means to be known by God. It means that we have nothing to hide or to fear for he is acquainted with us. He knows our skills and our ways of thinking. He is knowledgeable about the way we were taught and raised. He knows the things that will be an obstacle and hindrances in our path. This is why he is able to work all things out for our good. Nothing is hidden from him, therefore, he can make use of any circumstance to produce a good outcome if we are willing to usher in the good, focus on the good, highlight, and declare the good.

CRUCIFIXION CHALLENGE

"And we know that all things work together for good to them that love God, to them who are the called according to his purpose."
⚜ Romans 8:28

"Finally, brethren, whatsoever things are true, whatsoever things are honest, whatsoever things are just, whatsoever things are pure, whatsoever things are lovely, whatsoever things are of good report; if there be any virtue, and if there be any praise, think on these things."
⚜ Philippians 4:8

LESSON

Qadash is the Hebrew word for **sanctified**. It means to be prepared, dedicated, to be holy, separate, or to be hallowed. God placed a calling on Jeremiah from within his mother's womb to be holy. As we look deeper into the meaning of *qadash*, we learn that it also means to consecrate, to be pure and clean.

THE 21 DAY

In reality, God created a future for the prophet that was activated in Jeremiah 1:4 when the Word of the Lord came to Jeremiah. In order for that word to achieve its purpose, Jeremiah needed to consent and agree to the Word of God.

God placed a standard on the life of Jeremiah. Why?

"Because it is written, Be ye holy; for I am holy."
⚜ 1 Peter 1:16

As believers, we are called to be holy for God is holy. Christ is coming back for a church that is without spot or wrinkle. We are not to even have a blemish.

"That he might present it to himself a glorious church, not having spot, or wrinkle, or any such thing; but that it should be holy and without blemish."
⚜ Ephesians 5:27

CRUCIFIXION CHALLENGE

Amōmos is the Greek word for blemish and it means to be without faultiness, to be blameless and morally sound. In essence, it is to be without a hint, hue, or shadow of darkness.

MEDITATION

Are there areas in your life, which are, spots, faults, moral blemishes, or outright sins (2 Peter 2:13)? Are there wrinkles, issues or areas where you need to be delivered or rescued (Matthew 9:18-26)? Are there places in your life where you have a blot of disgrace and need it to be addressed by Jesus (John 8:5-10)?

The 6 MINUTE CHALLENGE

The challenge today is to identify any such areas and confess them to the Lord. Declare that as of this day you are free from the issue. That you will no longer allow the enemy to stain your life or witness with sin. Today you have been delivered from shame and disgrace.

THE 21 DAY

If you are not sure how to pray then trust Holy Spirit to pray for you. Pray in tongues and then with your conscious mind and let the declaration of your lips consent and agree to all that was uttered on your behalf.

PRAYER

Father, we thank you that you have made all provisions for us no matter what the issue. You have provided help for our infirmities, deliverance for oppression, new garments to cover our shame, and hope for despondence. In you, we have all that we need to *overcome*. Father, today we judge the works of the enemy as sinful, unrighteous, and unholy. We do not want to walk with him or partner with him in the name of Jesus.

CRUCIFIXION CHALLENGE

Our lips will speak words of life. We will declare the truth as you have spoken them to us. You formed us so we are strong. You knew us before therefore, we have no cause to wear shame. And you have sanctified us so that we can be holy as you are holy. Father, let your holiness manifest in us more fully in this season we pray, in Jesus name, amen.

CHALLENGE DAY 4

CREATED

FOR LIGHT

PRAYER

Father, we are thankful that you have sanctified us. You have called us to be separate and holy unto yourself. Father forgive us wherein we have sinned and fallen short. Cast our sins out into the sea of forgetfulness. Lord, we love your patience and your mercy, which covers us. We thank you for being faithful even when we are not. Give us the grace to live lives of holiness. May we be clean and pure before you and before all men in the mighty name of Jesus we pray, amen.

THE 21 DAY

SCRIPTURAL FOCUS

"Then the word of the LORD came unto me, saying, Before I formed thee in the belly I knew thee; and before thou camest forth out of the womb I sanctified thee, and I ordained thee a prophet unto the nations."

⚜ Jeremiah 1:4-5

Yesterday we learned what it means to be *sanctified* by God. As children of Jehovah, we are called to be holy and to live lives that distinguishes us from those who reside in the world (John 17:16). Although we literally dwell on the earth, we are to live as citizens of heaven Philippians 3:20). Our lives are to reflect the *qadash* of God. As we submit to the process of God, he will enable us to live pure and clean lives resulting in our becoming *amōmos* in God.

LESSON

Nathan is the Hebrew word for ordained. It means to give, put or to set. However, *Nathan* conveys the understanding of an appointment, to be assigned something, or to designate a thing. Woven into the word *Nathan* is the notion of infliction, the essence of creation where things are made, it speaks of being delivered up to a thing or to be given something by someone. Therefore, when God told Jeremiah that he was ordained God was informing Jeremiah of the magnitude of the call that was placed on his life before he was formed and before he came out from the womb!

In essence the mark of **light** was placed on Jeremiah similar to the great lights that God placed in the heavens to illuminate the earth (Genesis 1:17). The word *Nathan* was used in Genesis 1:17 for the word *set*. Jeremiah's call was to bring light, shed light, and to be light. As God set the lights in the firmament of heaven to give light to the earth, so he set Jeremiah to shine light on the earth.

THE 21 DAY

God has also called us to be lights in the earth. How can we be light if we doubt God? If we continually profess what we cannot do rather than establish what we can do through Christ Jesus?

Jeremiah was ordained to be a prophet to nations. He was to show them the light of God. In like manner so are we (Matthew 5:14, Acts 22:15, John 12:32). What does it mean to be a prophet? It means to be a *representative* or a *speaker* for God. Therefore, we are to speak words that lift up Christ as the light of the world so that men can be drawn to him.

Do your words draw men to Christ? Do they establish his sovereignty? Do they open the way for abundant life to be manifested continually in your life and in the lives of those around you?

MEDITATION

God has placed a call on your life. This means that your life is no longer yours. You are required to carry your cross

CRUCIFIXION CHALLENGE

for at any moment he can require that you die (to yourself, to your emotions, or to your thoughts). If you refuse, are you a new creature? If you hold on to your old man, have you crucified *self*? Are you *really* dead?

Dead people do not speak. Resurrected people will speak only the words given by the Lord and their words will bear witness to Jesus and uphold the kingdom of life.

Take time to reflect on your life. Have you died yet? Are you really resurrected in Christ Jesus? Are there still some things that need to be nailed to the cross? Are you ready to put them on the cross in order to walk in your ordination?

The 7 MINUTE CHALLENGE

With the guidance of Holy Spirit, pray over your list. Speak a word of death to anything that is unlike Christ in your life. Speak a word of death to those things that can separate you from the Lord. Speak a word of death to sinful

THE 21 DAY

thinking. Speak a word of death to lusts and affections. Speak death to the wrong emotions such as doubt, worry, fear, hatred, and jealousy.

"And they that are Christ's have crucified the flesh with the affections and lusts."
⚜ Galatians 5:24

Whatever does not die will fight against you! Whatever is not placed on the cross will once again yoke you in bondage (Galatians 5:1). The Bible is clear on the fact that if you try to preserve your life you will lose it. However, if you die for the sake of Christ you will find your life!

"He that findeth his life shall lose it: and he that loseth his life for my sake shall find it."
⚜ Matthew 10:39

CRUCIFIXION CHALLENGE

PRAYER

Our Father and our God, we have come confessing that we are weak and in so many instances, we are powerless to bring about the needed change in our members. The enemy is pressing his advantage to exploit our emotions, our thoughts, and to influence our actions. Father, we thank you for your grace, which is sufficient for us.

Father, pour out your grace upon us. Exercise your power in our situations. Father, help us as we face anger, as we deal with envy, as we speak death to lust, as we kill affections that would drive a wedge between us and you. Father hear us.

Father, we know that in order for us to move from glory to glory your power must be alive and active within us. Help us to activate and grow in the power of Christ. Father, as things die within us may the power of Christ grow stronger and the glory of God brighter in Jesus name we pray, amen.

THE 21 DAY

Father, may we nail hatred, discord, disbelief, anxiety, worry, and fear to the cross of Christ for they are not of the spirit of *light*.

Father, help us to obey. Help us to put all before you believing that the victory is ours for it was secured in the completed work of Christ. Father, let nothing shake us from this truth. Let nothing tarnish our testimony in Christ Jesus.
We bless you and thank you in Jesus name, amen.

"When God exercises his power he manifests his glory."
⚜ M.J. Welcome

May the Lord exercise his power within us so that his glory may manifest around us, in Jesus name, amen.

CHALLENGE DAY 5

RESPONSE

OF A CHILD

PRAYER

Father, may your grace cover us as we embark on day 5 of our challenge. Cause your grace to be sufficient to help us overcome all that we will battle today. Deeply root your Word in the good soil of our hearts, in the name of Jesus. Father, all glory is yours; all power is yours, all things in heaven and on earth are yours. May they reflect and represent you this day in Jesus name, amen.

THE 21 DAY

SCRIPTURAL FOCUS

"Then the word of the LORD came unto me, saying, Before I formed thee in the belly I knew thee; and before thou camest forth out of the womb I sanctified thee, and I ordained thee a prophet unto the nations. Then said I, Ah, Lord GOD! behold, I cannot speak: for I am a child."
⚜ Jeremiah 1:4-6

How wonderful it is to know that God has ordained us to be lights in the earth and to be his mouthpiece wherever we go. We have the ability to influence nations and to intercede on their behalf. We can follow in the footsteps of men like Jonah, Paul, and Elijah. However, our responsibility goes far beyond just speaking or recognizing God's call on our lives, it requires us to die to *self*. We are required to crucify everything that would keep us bound to the earth. We are to put to death all that Satan could use to sift us from God.

CRUCIFIXION CHALLENGE

There is no new life without death to the old life. With God, there is no partial death. Christ established the pattern for us. It must be all or nothing.

LESSON

Today's focus will be on Jeremiah 1:6. We will examine Jeremiah's response to the wondrous news God shared with the prophet. Jeremiah's response was similar to that of Moses and if we are honest probably similar to our own. When God pulls back the curtains and reveals his secrets to us, we often panic because we look at who we are and not at who he is. Here we see that Jeremiah did exactly that. The fact that Jeremiah raised the issue that he could not speak for he was a child indicates that the prophet was comparing himself to something or to someone. In his own estimation, he was incapable of doing the work assigned to him in spite of the fact God told him he was fashioned for the task that laid ahead of him.

Na`ar is the Hebrew word for *child*. It means lad, servant, a boy, or a youth. He was like a young lion just starting to rustle his mane or one who was just coming into himself. He was still inexperienced. He was able to roar, but still lacked the strength of an aged lion. He did not possess the skills necessary to survive and to hold territory in a sense. What does that sound like? Faith or fear, worry, with a splash of doubt?

Jeremiah had connected with God in such a way that the Word of the Lord came to him and because of this connection God revealed to him what Jeremiah had not known before. Maybe he was inquiring about his purpose. Maybe he desired to do something great for God. Maybe he complained to God about the sins of the people and wanted God to do something or say something. Yet when God spoke, Jeremiah retreated and hid behind inexperience and youthfulness. He lacked *confidence*.

CRUCIFIXION CHALLENGE

In this moment his love, dedication, and faith in God was being tested. Whom was he going to believe? If the discussion had ended there then Jeremiah would probably have abandoned the call of God. However, God corrected him. *"Say not, I am a child."*

Has God ever said those words to you? When you speak negative words over your life do you hear him speaking to you "Say not . . ." Or when you start to view yourself through the eyes of the world, the enemy, or others does God whisper corrective words to you?

Do you listen?

The prophet Jeremiah listened to the word of the Lord (Jeremiah 1:6-19). He did not say anything. He was silent. He allowed the Lord to do what needed to be done so that he could speak for Jehovah. Jeremiah's silence allowed God to fill his mouth with the Words of God. The lesson here is that if we keep talking God cannot place his

THE 21 DAY

words of power and light into our mouths.

When was the last time you were silent before God? When was the last time you allowed God to do in you what needed to be done so that you could fulfill his purpose in the earth? When was the last time you heard from God so clearly and believed him unwaveringly?

MEDITATION

"Stand in awe, and sin not: commune with your own heart upon your bed, and be still. Selah."
⚜ Psalms 4:4

"O that ye would altogether hold your peace! and it should be your wisdom."
⚜ Job 13:5

Take some time to commune with your heart. Are there areas where God has spoken words of revelation to you and you lifted excuses before him, as Moses and Jeremiah did? Has God ever

CRUCIFIXION CHALLENGE

given you an assignment to fulfil, and you ran away as Jonah did?

Are you ready to return to him? Are you ready for God to touch and fill your mouth? Do you want him to set you over nations and kingdoms, to enable you to root out and pull down, to throw down and destroy, to plant and build?

Jeremiah spoke again only to answer a direct question from the Lord (Jeremiah 1:11). Why did God ask him the question? God asked him the question to establish a fact that as surely as the almond tree is the first to blossom in springtime so too would his word. God gave Jeremiah a word that *rooted* him in confidence in Jehovah.

As you look at your life what do you see? What do you believe? What do you desire?

THE 21 DAY

"So shall my word be that goeth forth out of my mouth: it shall not return unto me void, but it shall accomplish that which I please, and it shall prosper in the thing whereto I sent it."

✝ Isaiah 55:11

The 8 MINUTE CHALLENGE

The challenge today is to spend 8 minutes in the presence of the Lord in order to sow a new beginning. Die to the old self. No more excuses. No more claiming inexperience, youthfulness, or lack of skill. Today, just surrender yourself to the Lord. Cry out for him to touch your mouth, to fill it with his words of life, which are powerful. Move the mountains of doubt and worry from your midst cast them into the sea. Dislodge the kingdom of Satan which is trying to establish death within your boarders though disbelief (Numbers 13:33).

The road to abundant life comes through faith, which comes from hearing the Word of God.

CRUCIFIXION CHALLENGE

"So then faith cometh by hearing, and hearing by the word of God."
⚜ Romans 10:17

When we hear our own negative words we are deaf, but when we perceive the Word of God and believe it, we move into a higher realm of hearing, which is infused with power, life, and supernatural ability. Are you ready to go up higher?

PRAYER

Father, your Word says that life and death is in the power of the tongue. Help us not to speak words of death to our destiny, our call, or over our victory in the name of Jesus. Teach us how to release words of truth and power over ourselves and over what you have placed under our charge. Help us to remain silent believing that what you have said is truth and that it will be the foundation upon which we build our house, in the name of Jesus.

THE 21 DAY

Father, let every other structure, which is built on falsehood, error, lies, or with the bricks of the enemy be torn down in the name of Jesus. Father, help us to accept that when the storms or trials of life come we will be safe and secure in structures, which were built by your divine hands.

Father, no matter what we face, give us the grace to rejoice over the blessing to *suffer* for the cause of Christ

"And they departed from the presence of the council, rejoicing that they were counted worthy to suffer shame for his name."
⚜ Acts 5:41

Father, cause our bodies to be glorious in the name of Jesus. Let us die so that we may live in the freedom that comes through Christ and him alone.

CRUCIFIXION CHALLENGE

"For our conversation is in heaven; from whence also we look for the Saviour, the Lord Jesus Christ: Who shall change our vile body, that it may be fashioned like unto his glorious body, according to the working whereby he is able even to subdue all things unto himself."
⚜ Philippians 3:20-21

We rejoice in the fact that it is done in the mighty name of Jesus, amen.

"And whatsoever ye shall ask in my name, that will I do, that the Father may be glorified in the Son."
⚜ John 14:13

CHALLENGE

DAY 6

GOD'S

TOUCH

PRAYER

Father, we thank you for our new course in life. We are no longer willing to speak words of *death*. We have resolved in our hearts that we will no longer make excuses. Father, we thank you for taking us up higher in you. Lord, we ask that every form of *corruption* will fall away from us in the name of Jesus. That the enemy will not be able to use our words against us. That the enemy will become *unemployed* in our lives in Jesus name we pray, amen.

THE 21 DAY

SCRIPTURAL FOCUS

"Then said I, Ah, Lord GOD! behold, I cannot speak: for I am a child. But the LORD said unto me, Say not, I am a child: for thou shalt go to all that I shall send thee, and whatsoever I command thee thou shalt speak. Be not afraid of their faces: for I am with thee to deliver thee, saith the LORD Then the LORD put forth his hand, and touched my mouth. And the LORD said unto me, Behold, I have put my words in thy mouth."
⚜ Jeremiah 1:6-9

Yesterday we learned the meaning of the word **Na`ar**. We are all children of God, however; we are fashioned and formed with supernatural ability. This is why age does not matter, education does not matter, and experience is not a prerequisite for us to be used for the purposes of God (1 Timothy 4:12).

Faith in God, obedience to God, and a willingness to go where God sends us are of the utmost importance. This is the reason that men like Timothy could do the work assigned to them in

CRUCIFIXION CHALLENGE

spite of their age. It is the reason why unlearned men could turn the world upside down for Christ (Acts 4:13). Or that men like Paul who pursued and murdered the innocent could be used mightily for the cause of the gospel (Acts 8:1, Acts 9:25-29).

"For all have sinned, and come short of the glory of God;"
✜ Romans 3:23

We have all fallen short of the glory that God originally intended for mankind. Yet he has opened the way for each of us to be restored to a state of glory, which will increase as we allow him to continue to shape and fashion us in the likeness of Christ Jesus (2 Corinthians 3:18).

LESSON

In Jeremiah 1:9, we learn that the Lord stretched forth his hand and touched Jeremiah's mouth. According to the Hebrew, word for touch ***naga*** ` God struck, applied, extended or reached toward Jeremiah's mouth. It has the understanding of reaching for something in order to injure or to violate it. It also means to smite or to beat a thing. The first use of *naga`* was in Genesis 3:3, when Eve recounted for the serpent the words of God.

"But of the fruit of the tree which is in the midst of the garden, God hath said, Ye shall not eat of it, neither shall ye touch it, lest ye die."
⚜ Genesis 3:3

We know that Eve did not quote God's words accurately. For God actually said,

"But of the tree of the knowledge of good and evil, thou shalt not eat of it: for in the day that thou eatest thereof thou shalt surely die."
⚜ Genesis 2:17

Eve added in the word *touch* and the penalty that associated with touching the fruit of the tree. God never told them that they could not touch the tree or the fruit of the tree. He specifically commanded them not to

CRUCIFIXION CHALLENGE

eat of the tree. The enemy used this opening to worm his way into Eve's reasoning. Why is this significant?

Eve was the mother of all living (Genesis 3:20) and as such the words she spoke lacked accuracy even before the fall. This is why she was *deceived*. She believe that what she said and thought was accurate and true. However, it was not. Similarly, there are things that we believe and hold on to that are not true nor are they accurate. There are things that come out of our mouths that we are convinced with our whole heart are factual, but they are not and they can open doors of deception.

Man's ability to misspeak or to embellish goes back to the beginning and finds its origin in the misspoken words of Eve. Maybe she was excited, zealous, or overly confident, whatever was behind her statement caused her to give the enemy an opening, which he seized and used it. It opened the way for her to eventually eat the fruit of the tree.

THE 21 DAY

This is the reason God had to reach out and touch Jeremiah's mouth. Jeremiah had misspoken. He stated he could not speak and the reason why was because he was a child. Although he believed the words that he spoke, God revealed to him that it was not true nor was it accurate.

It is significant that God touched Jeremiah's mouth. There was more to God's action than what is evident on the surface. What God did was a *violent* action. He smote the source of the words that flowed from the mouth of Jeremiah because his words were like poison. They were as dangerous as a disease. And if he continued to feed on them, they would produce death in him and for others.

Death and life are in the power of the tongue: and they that love it shall eat the fruit thereof."
⚜ Proverbs 18:21

CRUCIFIXION CHALLENGE

The root meaning for Hebrew word *peh* for *mouth* reveals the true significance of what transpired. *Peh* gets its meaning from *pa'ah*, which means to cleave in pieces, to shatter to dash to pieces or to break into pieces. This tells us that God came near; he got close to Jeremiah in order to break in pieces something that existed in him. In this case, it was the words or the declarations of his mouth. In order for Jeremiah to be used by God as a prophet and as a representative to nations, he needed accuracy and precision of words. Jeremiah's call was to speak words of power and life. Words that would make a difference to the survival of nations. There was no room for error or for him to misspeak therefore; God started at a simple, but pivotal place—Jeremiah's view of himself.

It is interesting that Eve's words distorted what God said as it misrepresented what she and Adam were directed not to do. This opened the way for the enemy to present them with a *different reality* of who they were to be. Satan painted a picture that seem to elevate them in glory and position for they would be *like* God in their own view, yet in reality they would fall in position because they were already like God because they were created in the image of God.

This is the tactic of the enemy. He listens to what we say in order to present us with a future, an aspiration, a desire that would appear to elevate us when in reality it sinks us deeper into the mire (John 10:10).

MEDITATION

Are you willing to let God draw near to you, to cleave to you in order to dash erroneous beliefs to pieces? Are you willing to let him shatter your words of death? Are you willing to let him smite you in order to redeem your calling?

The 9 MINUTE CHALLENGE

The number 9 signifies judgment. You have to make a decision. What will you do from this day on? Will you allow

CRUCIFIXION CHALLENGE

God to redeem *all* for you? Or will you allow the enemy to continue to dictate who you are? Will you allow your words to confine, limit, or hold you back from receiving the fullness that God has prepared for you?

Take 9 minutes to cry out, repent, and pray to the Lord. When you are finished, take time to seal it with gratitude and thanksgiving. Shower God with your love and appreciation.

PRAYER

Father, we thank you that you cleave unto us in order to shatter the things of the enemy. Thank you that even the things we build for ourselves you are able to break in pieces in order to fulfill your purpose in our lives.

THE 21 DAY

Lord, we glorify you because those whom you love you correct. Thank you for correction, in the name of Jesus.

"For whom the Lord loveth he chasteneth, and scourgeth every son whom he receiveth."
⚜ *Hebrews 12:6*

CHALLENGE

DAY 7

DEBT

OF LOVE

PRAYER

Father, we thank you that you have opened our eyes regarding the importance of accurate speech. We ask that you strike our mouths now and shatter anything that is not of you. Break in pieces every word of death. Fill our mouths with truth and life in the name of Jesus.

THE 21 DAY

As we embark on day seven of our challenge fill us with your spirit, open the way of wisdom unto us. Give us understanding and help us to increase in knowledge. May our hearts be fertile soil for the planting or your word in Jesus name amen.

SCRIPTURAL FOCUS

"Owe no man any thing, but to love one another: for he that loveth another hath fulfilled the law."
⚜ Romans 13:8

Yesterday we learned about Eve's mistake and Jeremiah's misguided words. We also learned how God corrected Jeremiah. As prophets or representative of God, it is important for us to speak the right words and have accurate beliefs. If we do not it opens a way for the enemy to ensnare us. Let us be sensitive to the correction of the Lord so that we can be firmly establish on solid ground.

CRUCIFIXION CHALLENGE

"Therefore whosoever heareth these sayings of mine, and doeth them, I will liken him unto a wise man, which built his house upon a rock: And the rain descended, and the floods came, and the winds blew, and beat upon that house; and it fell not: for it was founded upon a rock. And every one that heareth these sayings of mine, and doeth them not, shall be likened unto a foolish man, which built his house upon the sand: And the rain descended, and the floods came, and the winds blew, and beat upon that house; and it fell: and great was the fall of it."

⚜ Matthew 7:24-27

LESSON

For today's lesson, Holy Spirit has identified a crucial element in our ability to advance forward in the things of God. It is vital for accomplishing the purpose of God. It is the *debt of love*.

THE 21 DAY

The debt of love is not just an outward thing, which we give to others, it is an inward thing as well. We are called to love ourselves in order to be able to truly love our neighbor.

"And the second is like, namely this, Thou shalt love thy neighbour as thyself. There is none other commandment greater than these." Mark 12:31

How can we love others if we do not love ourselves? How can we love ourselves if we are not shown or taught what love is? Our parents may have taught us their version of love. Our spouses may have shared their type of love with us. We may have benefited from the love of good friends, but if they did not learn it from God, if they do not possess his love, it is a semblance of love and not the real McCoy.

This is why Christ gave us the command to love the Lord our God with all our heart, mind, soul and strength.

CRUCIFIXION CHALLENGE

"And thou shalt love the Lord thy God with all thy heart, and with all thy soul, and with all thy mind, and with all thy strength: this is the first commandment."
✤ Mark 12:30

The love that Christ is speaking of here is not one of sentiment or emotion. It is one that will cause us and to relinquish all to God. It is a love that says I trust you even unto death. And this is the true test of whether we love others and ourselves. Are we willing to die for them?

Many have been asked the same question throughout the ages. Daniel was asked this question by those who tried to trap him. Do you love your God so much that you are willing to disobey a royal command and risk death? Daniel said yes. Stephen was asked the same question and he chose to lay down his life. He even asked God to forgive those who stoned him (Acts 7:60). Could you have done the same?

THE 21 DAY

Abraham was asked the same question but in a different way. Do you really love me Abraham, are you willing to give up the son you longed for in order to obey me? Do I *really* have all your affection? Do you love me *above* your son? Abraham said yes.

Elijah had the question posed to him as well when Jezebel threatened his life. He chose to run (1 Kings 19:3). He did not want to die. He was not willing to give up his life, he desired to preserve it and God tried to get him to see what he had done by asking, what was he doing here (1 Kings 19:13). In Elijah's case, it exposed a few areas of concern, his unwillingness to die for the cause of God as other prophets had (Matthew 23:37) and his lack of faith that the Lord could prevent Jezebel from taking his life.

Our lives have been redeemed therefore they are no longer ours. We must be willing to lay them down. The command to love God is to supersede our natural affections for mother, father, child, or friend. God owns all

CRUCIFIXION CHALLENGE

therefore, we are to do and say as he directs us in order for us to fulfill our debt and to bring about victory.

"And they overcame him by the blood of the Lamb, and by the word of their testimony; and they loved not their lives unto the death."
✠ Revelation 12:11

MEDITATION

In life, we are tested and it can take various forms. Some tests are in financial; others health related, while others are familial. Some people are tested in all these areas at the same time. What is important about these tests is how we view them and how we react to them.

How do you view your tests? How do you respond to them? Are you willing to silently go through them and allow God to complete his work in you? Do you complain about the injustice of the whole event? Do you allow it to strip away your faith and erode your firm standing in God?

THE 21 DAY

Do you look for how these circumstances can help you fulfill the debt of love? How it helps you to love to God, love to yourself, and to love others? With the right perspective, you will be able to rejoice in your trails and sufferings.

"And they departed from the presence of the council, rejoicing that they were counted worthy to suffer shame for his name."
⚜ Acts 5:41

In order to overcome we have to die to *all*. If we do not die to *all* then we will not be able to overcome the enemy. The true power of the blood of Christ it enables us to die to ourselves so that we can truly live for God.

"He that findeth his life shall lose it: and he that loseth his life for my sake shall find it."
⚜ Matthew 10:39

CRUCIFIXION CHALLENGE

"And Jesus answered and said, Verily I say unto you, There is no man that hath left house, or brethren, or sisters, or father, or mother, or wife, or children, or lands, for my sake, and the gospel's, But he shall receive an hundredfold now in this time, houses, and brethren, and sisters, and mothers, and children, and lands, with persecutions; and in the world to come eternal life."
✤ Mark 29-30

When we lay down our lives physically and emotionally we are promised we will receive a hundredfold now in this time. When was the last time you tested God in this? If we try to hold on to the thing we will lose it, but if we give it up then we will gain it and more!

The 10 MINUTE CHALLENGE

Take some time to meditate in the spirit. Are there things that you have robbed God with? Have you denied him access to certain areas of your life, relationships, emotion, your being, and your strength?

THE 21 DAY

Do you owe others a debt of love? Do you need to speak words of truth to them? Words of correction? Do you need to lay down your life (give up your right to yourself, or having things your way, or to be right all the time) in order to live?

Christ went as a lamb to slaughter. He spoke not.

"He was oppressed, and he was afflicted, yet he opened not his mouth: he is brought as a lamb to the slaughter, and as a sheep before her shearers is dumb, so he openeth not his mouth."
⚜ Isaiah 53:7

When was the last time you were afflicted and kept your mouth shut? When was the last time you faced hardships and persecutions and remained silent?

For some of us, we owe ourselves the debt of love. We need to speak words of life to ourselves. We need to love ourselves, believe that we are valuable and that we count. We owe our bodies,

CRUCIFIXION CHALLENGE

our emotions, and our thoughts love for we have spoken words of hate, disgust, and bondage over ourselves for years. Today is the day where all of that can change.

"And above all things have fervent charity among yourselves: for charity shall cover the multitude of sins."
⚜ 1 Peter 4:8

Cover the sin with love. This is what God has provided for us. Use it to cover any sin Holy Spirit has identified. Decide to declare your love for yourself. Acknowledge that God is in the process of making you beautiful for your season (Ecclesiastes 3:11). The beauty of God is physical nor is it on the surface of our being. The glory of God surrounds our spiritual man, which radiates from the inside.

PRAYER

Oh thou God of love, we ask that you teach us how to love you with our whole heart, mind, soul, and strength. Help us to fulfill our debt of love to you

THE 21 DAY

in the name of Jesus. Lord, help us to fulfill the debt of love to ourselves that wherein we have not loved ourselves with a sacrificial love cause us to do so now. Where we have not spoken words of love and life to ourselves fill our mouths with it now. Help us to live lives that radiate and demonstrate your love from this point forward in the name of Jesus.

Lord, we desire to love our neighbors, teach us as you taught Christ. We want to learn obedience. Help us to view our suffering from your perspective, which is good and beneficial. Help us to ascend higher than the suffering or the trial. We desire for you to complete your perfection process in us to the glory of Christ Jesus.

"Though he were a Son, yet learned he obedience by the things which he suffered; And being made perfect, he became the author of eternal salvation unto all them that obey him;"
⚜ Hebrews 5:8-9

CRUCIFIXION CHALLENGE

Father, help us to be willing to die to ourselves so that our friends my live. Help us to love them in a way that forces us to tell them the truth and to correct them with gentleness and grace. Father, help us to act and operate in a way that will not cause them to fall or be lost. We rejoice in you for we have been counted worthy to suffer for the cause of Christ. Help us not to tarnish our witness, but to make it shine brightly before men so that you will be glorified in the name of Jesus.

Expose all darkness and increase the light that is inside and around us. Pierce the eyes of the blind and push back the kingdom of darkness as you cause us to shine brilliantly in the glory of God, we pray, amen.

CHALLENGE

DAY 8

LAYING

ASIDE ALL

PRAYER

Our Father who art in Heaven hollowed is your name. Lord, we thank you that you have enlightened us. We bless you because of your unfailing love. And we praise you because you are teaching us how to operate in your love and to shed your love on others and ourselves. Father, help us to fulfill our debt of love to all men. Show us how it looks and feels. Establish us in it so that we will never again speak, act, or operate with an unloving heart or spirit toward you, ourselves, or others, in Jesus name we pray, amen.

THE 21 DAY

SCRIPTURAL FOCUS

"But made himself of no reputation, and took upon him the form of a servant, and was made in the likeness of men: And being found in fashion as a man, he humbled himself, and became obedient unto death, even the death of the cross. Wherefore God also hath highly exalted him, and given him a name which is above every name: That at the name of Jesus every knee should bow, of things in heaven, and things in earth, and things under the earth; And that every tongue should confess that Jesus Christ is Lord, to the glory of God the Father."

⚜ Philippians 2:7-11

Yesterday we learned a lot about the debt of love. This may have been a challenging lesson to you, but the lesson is not over. It is lifelong. God will present opportunities for each of us to grow. He will hone our skills and will help to refine it for us. All we need to do is to be willing to learn and submit to his process. If we do, we will emerge as pure and tested gold.

CRUCIFIXION CHALLENGE

LESSON

Today's lesson focuses on the phrase *"no reputation."* What does that convey to us? What does it mean? What did it involve? And is this the template of life we are to follow? And if we are what will it look like for us?

Kenoō is the Hebrew word for ***reputation.*** It means to empty, make void, to deprive of force, to render vain, of no effect, or useless. It is to be empty handed, without a gift, to be vain of purpose or to be a vessel that contains nothing. The word, *no* which proceeds the word *reputation* is what gives *kenoō* its meaning therefore, it is already in its negative form.

Jesus laid aside his power, his position, his standing with God, and became an empty vessel in order that he could model the way to become filled by the presence of God. He came as a baby and he learned obedience. He slowly and methodically was filled with the presence of God. Christ came without a gift for he was the *gift of God.* Christ

THE 21 DAY

was not the owner of the gift God was. He came without his own purpose, because he only came to do the will of the Father so he did not have a personal agenda. God's agenda ruled and guided Jesus' life, actions, thoughts, words, and desires.

"For I came down from heaven, not to do mine own will, but the will of him that sent me."
⚜ John 6:38

"For I have not spoken of myself; but the Father which sent me, he gave me a commandment, what I should say, and what I should speak."
⚜ John 12:49

"Then answered Jesus and said unto them, Verily, verily, I say unto you, The Son can do nothing of himself, but what he seeth the Father do: for what things soever he doeth, these also doeth the Son likewise."
⚜ John 5:19

CRUCIFIXION CHALLENGE

Christ took on the form, the external appearance of a servant. This means that he was willing to be regarded, respected, and viewed as a servant. He tolerated the snares, jabs, ridicule, and insults that went with the lowly position as well (Matthew 13:55, John 1:46). He did not just come in the likeness of men, but in the form of the lowest of men. He came as one who appeared weak and without power. A person who serve others of higher positions. In a sense, Christ put on a disguise for he was not powerless nor was he a person without position or authority (Matthew 26:53). Yet he appeared to be so to those who looked with temporal and earthly eyes.

As his followers, we are called to be of *no reputation*. Yet this is an area in which many of us struggle. We refuse to lay aside our reputation. We find it insulting if we are not respected or honored. It is difficult to stomach being viewed or treated as less than. We take pride in our positions, titles, and accomplishments. We desire to be

THE 21 DAY

men of renown here and now (Genesis 6:4, Matthew 6:1-21).
Why is that?

It comes from the same thing that enticed Adam and Eve in the garden.

"For God doth know that in the day ye eat thereof, then your eyes shall be opened, and ye shall be as gods, knowing good and evil."
⚜ Genesis 3:5

It is the desire to be *great*. To be better than what we are or who we are outside of God. The way that God makes us great is not the way the world does it. In the world if you are wealthy, successful, have high numbers (sales, followers, church members, books published), or won awards you are viewed as a person with *reputation*. A person of honor, one that should be respected.

"For what shall it profit a man, if he shall gain the whole world, and lose his own soul?"
⚜ Mark 8:36

CRUCIFIXION CHALLENGE

God chooses to honor those who are nothing, who empty themselves out in order that he can fill them with himself (Matthew 5:5). He exalts those who are willing to endure disrespect, snide words, hurtful comments, injustices in order to obtain what he has laid in front of them. He honors those who are willing to forget about earthly accolades in order to hear his precious words well done John 3:35, John 5:20, John 13:3).

"Wherefore the LORD God of Israel saith, I said indeed that thy house, and the house of thy father, should walk before me for ever: but now the LORD saith, Be it far from me; for them that honour me I will honour, and they that despise me shall be lightly esteemed."
⚜ 1 Samuel 2:30

"Whosoever therefore shall confess me before men, him will I confess also before my Father which is in heaven."
⚜ Matthew 10:32

THE 21 DAY

"If any man serve me, let him follow me; and where I am, there shall also my servant be: if any man serve me, him will my Father honour."
⚜ John 12:26

In order to achieve God's highest purposes we must be willing to take on the form of a servant just as Christ did. To become like the *gift of God*. We are to trust God and allow him to form us, guide us, teach us, and direct us. If he says, shed this then we are to lay it aside. If he says, die to that we are to say yes Lord. If he says, forgo any awards we are to obey and say absolutely!

Is it easy? No, it is not! Is it required? It is! Christ learned to be obedient to the Father therefore, so must we.

"Though he were a Son, yet learned he obedience by the things which he suffered; And being made perfect, he became the author of eternal salvation unto all them that obey him;"
⚜ Hebrews 5:8-9

CRUCIFIXION CHALLENGE

MEDITATION

Are you willing to lay aside your reputation for the cause of Christ? Are you willing to become nothing? To be viewed as nothing? To have nothing in order to gain everything God has for you?

How do you feel inside right now, as you contemplate the questions asked? Are you at peace? Is something rising up inside of you screaming no way? Has your rational mind began to speak saying you can have both. You do not have to give up a thing.

Pay close attention to the words that are speaking in your mind right now. Write them out. Listen to the words of your heart note them. Examine your feelings and emotions note them. These are all indications that you could be in danger. It could be exposing that you have an enemy in your camp or that there is an idol in the midst.

THE 21 DAY

The 11 MINUTE CHALLENGE

The number 11 represents disorder, disorganization, imperfection, and disintegration according to E. W. Bullinger (http://www.electforum.com/Number%20in%20Scripture.pdf).

This means that you have the opportunity to topple what the enemy has tried to build within you. You can shatter his ideas and notions, you can expose and dispose of his schemes and plans, you can make his edifice in you crumble and collapse. You can bring about dissolution right now in the name of Jesus!

Take 11 minutes to pray to the Lord in the spirit or with your natural tongue, and topple the things you discovered are causing you to hold on to your earthly reputation. Ask the Lord to form you as a servant so that you can fulfill your mission of being the *gift of God* so that others will see your light and come into the household of faith.

CRUCIFIXION CHALLENGE

PRAYER

Father, I thank you for your faithfulness toward me. I bless you that in you I am able to be all things. I lay aside my reputation Lord and I ask you to help me become nothing so that in you I can be more than I would be without you.

Father, take my hand and lead me in the way I am to go. Help me so that I will never depart from it. Help me to crucify my old desires to be great without your guidance. Help me to lay all at the cross of Christ. Let it be dead unto me I pray, in Jesus name, amen.

CHALLENGE DAY 9

HUMBLENESS

PAVES THE WAY

PRAYER

Father, we thank you that you are teaching and leading us by your Spirit. We ask that you help us to advance and to never retreat in the name of Jesus. Help us to live the words of Christ, "not our will but thine be done." Father, help us not to be pretenders, but genuine articles for the kingdom of God we pray, amen.

THE 21 DAY

SCRIPTURAL FOCUS

"But made himself of no reputation, and took upon him the form of a servant, and was made in the likeness of men: And being found in fashion as a man, he humbled himself, and became obedient unto death, even the death of the cross. Wherefore God also hath highly exalted him, and given him a name which is above every name: That at the name of Jesus every knee should bow, of things in heaven, and things in earth, and things under the earth; And that every tongue should confess that Jesus Christ is Lord, to the glory of God the Father."
⚜ Philippians 2:7-11

Yesterday we learned about *humbleness* and what it entails. We discovered that the enemy uses the same familiar tactics because they work. We also took time to observe and examine our reactions to see if there were any warning signs we should pay attention to and address. We learned that if we gain the reputation that we strive for, the one that man and the world bestows on us

CRUCIFIXION CHALLENGE

it will be meaningless and worthless if God calls us wicked.

"And then will I profess unto them, I never knew you: depart from me, ye that work iniquity."
⚜ Matthew 7:23

No one will vouch for us in hell. God will not read our resumes or acknowledge our degrees. He will not hold us in high esteem because we had houses, land, or cars! There will be only one thing of interest to him. Did we completely obey Jesus? Did we follow the leading and guidance of Holy Spirit? Did we submit to the process in obedience?

LESSON

Philippians 2:8 points out key elements to fulfilling the call of God on our lives. Truthfully, these are the prerequisites to obtaining the reward or prize of God. The ability to humble oneself is pivotal. Becoming obedient unto death is another. And the final

THE 21 DAY

thing is allow what needs to be crucified to be crucified.

It is our responsibility to humble ourselves. This does not mean we should become doormats for others. It means to bring our selves low, reduce ourselves to meager circumstances, or to bring down our pride. It is to behave in an unassuming manner and to be devoid of all *haughtiness*. The Hebrew word ***tapeinos*** captures the essence of *humbleness*. It is to be lowly in spirit and to remain close to the ground. It conveys the notion of being brought low with grief, and deferring servilely to others.

It is not God's responsibility to humble us, but rather it is ours!

"Humble yourselves in the sight of the Lord, and he shall lift you up."
⚜ James 4:10

"Humble yourselves therefore under the mighty hand of God, that he may exalt you in due time:"
⚜ 1 Peter 5:6

CRUCIFIXION CHALLENGE

It is not impossible for God to humble the proud for he has done it in the past. Rulers like Pharaoh and Nebuchadnezzar can testify to the fact that Jehovah was and is able to humble the proud.

"But he giveth more grace. Wherefore he saith, God resisteth the proud, but giveth grace unto the humble."
⚜ James 4:6

"Surely he scorneth the scorners: but he giveth grace unto the lowly."
⚜ Proverbs 3:34

Although God could humble us himself, why would we want him to do so? Why would we prefer to have him force us into lowering ourselves or killing our pride? Would it not be better for us if we chose to do it? Cain chose not to humble himself when he spoke with God. It resulted in separation from his family. Cain was used as a warning to believers in 1 John 3:12.

THE 21 DAY

"Not as Cain, who was of that wicked one, and slew his brother. And wherefore slew he him? Because his own works were evil, and his brother's righteous."
⚜ 1 John 3:12

Pharaoh ended up at the bottom of the sea. Where do you want to end up? Do you want the honor you can give to yourself or the honor that comes from God?

The road to humbleness is the path of the cross!

"Then said Jesus unto his disciples, If any man will come after me, let him deny himself, and take up his cross, and follow me."
⚜ Matthew 16:24

It is being prepared and willing at any moment to defer your will, to relinquish your rights, to bite your tongue, to forgo an argument, to appear foolish in the eyes of others, to appear weak and useless all in order to be obedient to God, even if it means *death.*

CRUCIFIXION CHALLENGE

Death to your dreams, aspirations, wants, desires, lusts, and cravings. It means giving up chocolate if God asks you. It means washing yourself in the dirty water seven times if God says you should (2 Kings 5:10-14). It means lying on your left side for as long as God directs you to do so (Ezekiel 4:4). Or baking your bread with cow dung instead of human dung because the Lord told you to do it (Ezekiel 4:12-15). It is allowing God to use you as an instrument in order to confound the wise and mighty.

"But God hath chosen the foolish things of the world to confound the wise; and God hath chosen the weak things of the world to confound the things which are mighty;"
⚜ 1 Corinthians 1:27

MEDITATION

The Bible tells us that Jesus washed the filthy feet of his disciples. Imagine the King of Kings, the creator of all, the son of the living God stooping to wash your feet. I am sure that his flesh rebelled. His mind screamed. His heart spoke, his muscles resisted yet he commanded them to come under obedience to God the Father. He silenced their rebellion. He squashed their mutiny in order to fulfill his assignment.

When was the last time you washed someone's feet who was not a child or a baby? When was the last time you got on your knees in order to be of service to another?

Is the idea ridiculous, repulsive, disgraceful? This is what Christ did for us and it is what he expects us to do for others. It is easy to be served, but it is challenging to be of service.

If we truly humble ourselves, God will exalt us. The first step is ours and the final reward will come at the appearing of Christ.

"And when the chief Shepherd shall appear, ye shall receive a crown of glory that fadeth not away."
⚜ 1 Peter 5:4

CRUCIFIXION CHALLENGE

This does not mean that God will not honor us here on earth. For he could but we are assured if we complete the race set before us we will receive a crown of glory at the appearing of Christ

The 12 MINUTE CHALLENGE

The number 12 represents the perfection of the kingdom of God. Do you want the kingdom of God to be perfected in you, your members, and in your life? If so, take 12 minutes to cry out for it. Establish it. Covet it.

Ask God to present opportunities for you to humble yourself. For you to wash the feet of others. Ask him to help you to allow those who are willing to wash your feet and for them to serve you as well.

Sometimes it can be hard to allow others to do for us when we cannot do for ourselves. When old age or disability sets in our *pride* can take a big hit and we want to try to do all for ourselves. This is not God's way. There is a season for everything under the sun. There is a time where we can help others and there is a time when others are to help us. *Shame* is a powerful hindering force as well. It also finds life in pride. They both focus on *self*.

When you allow another to be of service to you, you are helping them to work out their salvation. It opens the way for them to fulfill the second command of Christ (Mark 12:30-31). When you tell them no, you deny them the opportunity to contribute the health and welfare of the kingdom of God.

Is there someone you can allow to help you with a task? Is there someone you can help with a task? Remember all things are subject to the leading of Holy Spirit so consult the Godhead before you run headlong into a situation. If you seek them, you will get the discernment and wisdom in order for you to proceed.

CRUCIFIXION CHALLENGE

PRAYER

Lord, the devil is crafty and we are unlearned. Help us not to be entangled in the yoke of bondage again. Keep us free from shame and help us not to walk in pride. Help us not to be ensnared by doubt, fear, or worry. Lord, keep us from being assimilated into Satan's kingdom in the name of Jesus.

Establish your *kingdom of light* in the deepest recesses of our being. Father, open every chamber within us and help us to evict what needs be evicted, to tear down and topple every foreign entity, help us to cover every sin and generational sin under the blood of Jesus, help us to break every curse and generational curse in Jesus name. We ask that every opening will be closed unto the enemy right now. You are the strongman who enables us to clean out your temple and furnish it with the things of the most high God. Let it not be vacant in Jesus name we pray, amen (Matthew 12:29, Luke 11:24-25, 1 Corinthians 3:16-17).

CHALLENGE

DAY 10

OBEDIENCE

UNTO DEATH

PRAYER

Lord, we come before you again in *humbleness* of spirit. We ask that everything that would raise itself up will be brought low in the name of Jesus. We pull down vain imaginations. We tear down haughty and boastful attitudes. We eliminate everything in our members that would dishonor your name.

THE 21 DAY

We need you to lift us up. We need you to exalt us in due season. We need you to make us *incorruptible*. Help us to stay the course and to bring you glory, in Jesus name we pray, amen.

SCRIPTURAL FOCUS

"But made himself of no reputation, and took upon him the form of a servant, and was made in the likeness of men: And being found in fashion as a man, he humbled himself, and became obedient unto death, even the death of the cross. Wherefore God also hath highly exalted him, and given him a name which is above every name: That at the name of Jesus every knee should bow, of things in heaven, and things in earth, and things under the earth; And that every tongue should confess that Jesus Christ is Lord, to the glory of God the Father."
⚜ Philippians 2:7-11

Yesterday we focused on *humbleness* and the benefits associated with taking a humble position before God. From a worldly perspective, it seems foolish to walk in humbleness but in

CRUCIFIXION CHALLENGE

reality, humbleness expresses the greatest strength. Only a person who is strong can truly be humble. A strength that comes from character, moral firmness, and steadfastness in a divine cause. Christ was never a weak man nor an impotent God, yet he walked in humbleness before all.

LESSON

Today's lesson will focus on part of Philippians 2:8, "... *and became obedient unto death, even the death of the cross.*"

The Bible tells us that Christ became obedient unto death, even the death of the cross. When we dissect the words in the phrase, we learn that Jesus went through a process of becoming obedient. He achieved this through practice, exercise, and use (Hebrews 5:8, 14). He listened and harkened to the command of God as far as or until the point of death. He went the complete length that God set for him. He did not stop short or abandon the cause of God when things got tough.

THE 21 DAY

Nor did he utilize his strength in order to change the situation. In addition, he did not open his mouth to complain about what was happening to him. *"He was oppressed and afflicted, yet He did not open His mouth. Like a lamb led to the slaughter and like a sheep silent before her shearers, He did not open His mouth."* Isaiah 53:7

This is an interesting notion because here we clearly see that Christ put aside his might, his strength, his right to life, and his right to survive in order to obey God. His obedience was **true** worship for he gave all of his substance in order to honor God.

In the natural when men are faced with death they fight to survive. They claw, kick, scream, wrestle, deny, pray, hope, and beg for their lives to be speared. Most people want to continue living and will use all at their disposal to ensure the continuance of their lives. Christ did not. He knew that in order for us to live he had to die. Therefore, he accepted the mission of God and he set his eyes on the Father and on him alone in order to complete his assignment.

As Creator, Christ possessed ability, power, and might yet he did not use it. He depended solely on what the Father gave to him and patiently waited for the time in which God saw fit to give him what was needed to address every situation. Likewise as followers of Christ, we are to worship God with our strength by laying it aside in obedience to Christ. We are to wait to be shown what to do or be willing to change direction when corrected by the Lord.

There are those who are able to accomplish great feats in life yet they attribute their ability and might to their trainer, to their own hard work, or to their lineage when in reality, God is the one who created them and he endowed them with abilities. God does not take back the gifts he gives (Romans 11:29). He waits for us to *freely* give them back to him. He wants us to honor him with them. When we give, others credit for our abilities or strengths we are in reality robbing God

THE 21 DAY

of what belongs to him. We are crowning the *creature* above the ***creator***.

"Saying with a loud voice, Worthy is the Lamb that was slain to receive power, and riches, and wisdom, and strength, and honour, and glory, and blessing."
⚜ Revelation 5:12

"Saying, Amen: Blessing, and glory, and wisdom, and thanksgiving, and honour, and power, and might, be unto our God for ever and ever. Amen."
⚜ Revelation 7:12

Each morning God blesses us with strength. We are able to open our eyes, get out of our beds, dress ourselves, brush our teeth, yet all too often we forget to honor God with our strength by saying thanks. We fail to acknowledge that he is the source of all that we are able to do and achieve. Somewhere along the line, we begin to believe that we can subsistent without him. Of course, we would never say it to him or others, yet our actions bear it out (Ecclesiastes 2:24).

CRUCIFIXION CHALLENGE

We will do for ourselves until we cannot then we will ask God for assistance. This is not the example of Christ. Christ could have done for himself, but he chose not to. He chose to live a life of dependence and reliance on God. Thus, he established for us the precedent of how we are to honor God. Although we can do certain things for ourselves, we are to make them subject to his will. Even when we can accomplish tasks independently, we should inquire if this is the best course of action. Giving God honor, worship, praise, and glory not only takes place in a church, but in our earthen temples (bodies). Our worship is to be daily and continual. We are called to be living sacrifices unto God (Romans 12:1).

Encapsulated in our bodies are hosts of things that belong to God. Our hearts, souls, strength and mind belongs to him therefore we are to worship him completely with them. By doing so we establish our love for him.

THE 21 DAY

"And he answering said, Thou shalt love the Lord thy God with all thy heart, and with all thy soul, and with all thy strength, and with all thy mind; and thy neighbour as thyself."
⚜ Luke 10:27

When we think like God this is a form of *worship*. When we speak like God, we *honor* him. When we use our strength properly, we crown him with *glory*. When we allow our souls to be transformed (prosper in the ways of God) this *blesses* him. When we are mindful of his beneficence, we give him *thanksgiving*.

However, when we boast on our accomplishments, degrees, abilities, or luck we are thieves since we are taking credit for what God has done and has enabled us to do.

The root of all is God thus there is nothing that exists or comes into being that is not rooted in him. For he is the beginning of life. All that is, originated in him! Therefore, the wise will give God the honor, glory, and praise now

CRUCIFIXION CHALLENGE

freely because the time is coming when he will demand it from everyone.

"For it is written, As I live, saith the Lord, every knee shall bow to me, and every tongue shall confess to God."
⚜ Romans 14:11

"That at the name of Jesus every knee should bow, of things in heaven, and things in earth, and things under the earth; And that every tongue should confess that Jesus Christ is Lord, to the glory of God the Father."
⚜ Philippians 2:10-11

MEDITATION

Have you robbed God? Have you taken credit for what God has done? Do you worship him with your strength, talents, and abilities? Does it go deeper than surface worship or pleasant sounding words?

THE 21 DAY

The 13 MINUTE CHALLENGE

Are you willing to become obedient unto death? Are you willing to go as far as the cross? Are you ready to worship God with your strength, mind, heart, and soul? Do you know how to do so?

The process is hidden in Christ Jesus and God determines it! Holy Spirit will lead and guide us if we are willing. Pour out your all to the Lord today. Spend 13 minutes in the presence of God confessing, repenting, and seeking the Lord's instructions. Offer him your strength. Lay down your wisdom, wealth, honor, glory, power, blessings, and thanksgiving before him. All that has been shed on you give it to him. He alone deserves it.

"Saying with a loud voice, Worthy is the Lamb that was slain to receive power, and riches, and wisdom, and strength, and honour, and glory, and blessing."
⚜ Revelation 5:12

CRUCIFIXION CHALLENGE

"Saying, Amen: Blessing, and glory, and wisdom, and thanksgiving, and honour, and power, and might, be unto our God for ever and ever. Amen."
⚜ Revelation 7:12

Thou art worthy, O Lord, to receive glory and honour and power: for thou hast created all things, and for thy pleasure they are and were created."
⚜ Revelation 4:11

PRAYER

Father, we give you honor and worship for the simple things in life. We bless you that you have given us strength to open our eyes, to scratch our backs, even to smile. We bless you that you have showered us with ability and skill. Lord, we receive it with thankful hearts and we offer it back to you. Wherein we have stolen glory that belonged to you, we ask that you forgive us. If we have robbed you of honor, we ask that you do not hold it against us.

THE 21 DAY

Lord, we submit to the process of becoming obedient. Help us to be patient with others and ourselves. Let us not rush the process but wait on you to do what is pleases you. Lord, we do not want to do lip service, but we want to be transformed from the heart level. We desire that our minds are renewed and that our souls begin to prosper as you intend them to and not as we desire. We ask these things in the matchless name of Jesus, amen.

CHALLENGE

DAY 11

ABILITY

TO INFLUENCE

PRAYER

Father, we thank for setting us on the course of obedience. We bless you for you have called us unto yourself. Thank you for fashioning us for your purpose. Lord, we break every agreement with our former selves and former lives. We embrace the life you have destined for us since the beginning of time.

Father, we ask you to touch our mouths and purify them. We ask that you strengthen our hearts so we faint not or become weary. Increase our patience and bestow on us a spirit of discernment so we can see and understand what is going on in and around us.

Let us not be mockery in the earth, but that we will be established as bright lights in Jesus name we pray, amen.

SCRIPTURAL FOCUS

"Saying with a loud voice, Worthy is the Lamb that was slain to receive power, and riches, and wisdom, and strength, and honour, and glory, and blessing."
⚜ Revelation 5:12

"Saying, amen: Blessing, and glory, and wisdom, and thanksgiving, and honour, and power, and might, be unto our God for ever and ever. amen."
⚜ Revelation 7:12

Thou art worthy, O Lord, to receive glory and honour and power: for thou hast created all things, and for thy pleasure they are and were created."
⚜ Revelation 4:11

CRUCIFIXION CHALLENGE

Yesterday we learned about how to worship God with our *strength*. The key to genuine worship is *obedience*. Obedience is a process which each of us must go through. It is not comprised of lessons we give ourselves but rather lessons that are given to us by God. We will undergo a *forging* process that will strengthen and purify us; at the same time, it will cause us to become brighter.

The fulfillment of this process requires that we give up everything that we have a right to legally. Our bodies, minds, conversations, habits, emotions, behaviors, and work ethics (Ephesians 4). Everything about us has to be transformed because it no longer belongs to us but to Christ.

"What? know ye not that your body is the temple of the Holy Ghost which is in you, which ye have of God, and ye are not your own?"
⚜ 1 Corinthians 6:19

THE 21 DAY

"Let this mind be in you, which was also in Christ Jesus:"
⚜ Philippians 2:5

"That ye put off concerning the former conversation the old man, which is corrupt according to the deceitful lusts; And be renewed in the spirit of your mind; And that ye put on the new man, which after God is created in righteousness and true holiness. Wherefore putting away lying, speak every man truth with his neighbour: for we are members one of another."
⚜ Ephesians 4:22-25

When we allow the process to proceed without interference, we *honor* God. When we submit to the process with obedience, we *worship* him.

LESSON

According to the Greek definition of **power**, it is possessing strength and ability in various areas, such as in one's nature, the ability to perform miracles, and in moral fortitude. It is having excellence of the soul, the

CRUCIFIXION CHALLENGE

ability to influence because of riches or wealth, by force because of hosts or armies. It is reflected in ones state of mind, by law, or custom. In every area where *power* can be displayed or exerted Jesus is worthy of receiving the credit for and in, that area from those who he has operated as an attendant.

Therefore, as believers when we are able to influence others for God, Christ is to get the credit. When we are able to perform miracles, it is to the glory of the Son. When we are able to stand morally in the midst of temptation, or to rule our souls with excellence according to the standard of God, Christ is to get the credit, for it demonstrates and testifies that his power enables us to do and accomplish all that we do.

What happens if we fail to operate with the correct spiritual attitude or perspective? Will we be unable to exercise the power of God? (Matthew 7:21-23)

THE 21 DAY

"And John answered and said, Master, we saw one casting out devils in thy name; and we forbad him, because he followeth not with us. And Jesus said unto him, Forbid him not: for he that is not against us is for us." Luke 9:49-50

"Many will say to me in that day, Lord, Lord, have we not prophesied in thy name? and in thy name have cast out devils? and in thy name done many wonderful works? And then will I profess unto them, I never knew you: depart from me, ye that work iniquity."
⚜ Matthew 7:22-23

Many will exercise power in the name of Jesus; however, they will not enter the kingdom of heaven. The kingdom of heaven is reserved only for those who do the will of the Father. In order to accomplish the will of the Father we have to become obedient unto death even in our exercising of the power bestowed to us.

Christ was given all power and he delegated a portion of that power to us.

CRUCIFIXION CHALLENGE

"And Jesus came and spake unto them, saying, All power is given unto me in heaven and in earth."
⚜ Matthew 28:18

"Behold, I give unto you power to tread on serpents and scorpions, and over all the power of the enemy: and nothing shall by any means hurt you."
⚜ Luke 10:19

We are responsible to remember the source of our power. We are to credit him and honor him with the power. And our usage of the power is to be subject to the will of God.

"Not every one that saith unto me, Lord, Lord, shall enter into the kingdom of heaven; but he that doeth the will of my Father which is in heaven."
⚜ Matthew 7:21

MEDITATION

Have you given God worship with your power? Have you utilized it to tread on serpents and scorpions or to overpower the enemy? Have you

THE 21 DAY

honored God by stripping Satan of his power or influence over your life, in trying situations, in your body, over the lives of friends, and relatives?

Have you sought God about the best way to use the power so that the enemy's attempts are rendered useless?

The 14 MINUTE CHALLENGE

Many have given up the fight. They have conceded the battle to the enemy. Their words and hearts bear witness against them. They are downcast and feel hopeless. If you are one of those people, you can be renewed today by the power of God!

Take 14 minutes and ask the Lord to replace your batteries. If they do not need to be replaced, ask him to recharge them in the name of Jesus.

Others may have taken credit for casting out demons, healing the sick, capturing, or freeing territory. Being so excited about the victory, we could

CRUCIFIXION CHALLENGE

have failed to notice that the enemy caused us to forget that the victory *belongs* to the Lord (Proverbs 21:31). Satan subtly placed his kingdom over us so that it would block light and cause us to start to exist and operate in the shadows. He blew a spirit of forgetfulness on us as he increased our excitement over the *miracle*. For he knows that if we remain focused on the miracle or the ability to operate in power then we will lose focus on what is important.

"And the seventy returned again with joy, saying, Lord, even the devils are subject unto us through thy name."
⚜ Luke 10:17

"Notwithstanding in this rejoice not, that the spirits are subject unto you; but rather rejoice, because your names are written in heaven."
⚜ Luke 10:20

What has your focus? What is it that excites you? The gift or ability? Or is it the fact that your name is written in heaven? How often do you give God

THE 21 DAY

thanks for including your name in his wondrous book?

PRAYER

All power belongs to you and you alone, oh Lord. Thank you for giving us the ability to utilize *your* power to the glory of the Father. We ask that you will help us to keep the right focus. We ask that you set your kingdom over us. Over our homes, minds, and hearts. May our motivations, celebrations, and rejoicing be rooted in what is pure and good. Father, help us to focus on you and not on our abilities. Lord let not the devil deceive us. Let him not lure us away with cleaver tricks or antics.

Helps us to remain alert and wise to his schemes and devices. We thank you that you are ever with us. We bless you for enabling us to stand and not fall prey to the enemy. We honor you, in Jesus name amen.

CHALLENGE

DAY 12

THE VALUE

OF TRUE RICHES

PRAYER

Lord, you have equipped us with your power. We have been given the weapons of God that are *mighty*. Father, the same weapons that you use you have entrusted to us. Help us to use them. Help us to believe. Help us to be effective. In all that we do we want to honor you. Father, we desire to give you want is rightly yours. Teach us we pray, amen.

THE 21 DAY

SCRIPTURAL FOCUS

"Saying with a loud voice, Worthy is the Lamb that was slain to receive power, and riches, and wisdom, and strength, and honour, and glory, and blessing."
⚜ Revelation 5:12

"Saying, amen: Blessing, and glory, and wisdom, and thanksgiving, and honour, and power, and might, be unto our God for ever and ever. amen."
⚜ Revelation 7:12

Thou art worthy, O Lord, to receive glory and honour and power: for thou hast created all things, and for thy pleasure they are and were created."
⚜ Revelation 4:11

Yesterday we learned about *power*. God has blessed us for we can exercise the power of God in the way we think and in the way; our souls prosper in the ways of God. Power is not just for signs, wonders, or miracles. God has given us power so that we can live *victorious* lives in him. There is no habit or addiction that we are

CRUCIFIXION CHALLENGE

incapable of mastering or breaking when we apply the power that God has given us!

We truly can do all things though Christ Jesus for he has given us the power to *overcome* at all times. The choice is ours whether we will walk with him and use all that he has bestowed on us.

LESSON

Riches according to the Greek meaning of the word is abundance, wealth, and fullness. It refers to a good, with which one is enriched. The root meaning of *riches* is to be filled up as in something that was once empty. Therefore, as believers we were empty vessels which have been filled with the essence of God through the work of the Son Christ Jesus. Let it be known, we are rich and wealthy only through Christ Jesus.

THE 21 DAY

To be rich, is to understand the source of all riches. It is to recognize that true riches comes through Christ Jesus. It is not about material possessions. The Laodicean church thought they were rich according to the words of Christ in Revelation 3:14-19, but in actuality they were a poor and wretched church.

"And unto the angel of the church of the Laodiceans write; These things saith the amen, the faithful and true witness, the beginning of the creation of God; I know thy works, that thou art neither cold nor hot: I would thou wert cold or hot. So then because thou art lukewarm, and neither cold nor hot, I will spue thee out of my mouth. Because thou sayest, I am rich, and increased with goods, and have need of nothing; and knowest not that thou art wretched, and miserable, and poor, and blind, and naked: I counsel thee to buy of me gold tried in the fire, that thou mayest be rich; and

CRUCIFIXION CHALLENGE

white raiment, that thou mayest be clothed, and that the shame of thy nakedness do not appear; and anoint thine eyes with eyesalve, that thou mayest see. As many as I love, I rebuke and chasten: be zealous therefore, and repent."
⚜ Revelation 3:14-19

The *lukewarm* referred in the scripture is that the Laodiceans were moving in the wrong direction. Rather than becoming hotter, through their relationship with Christ they were becoming cold. They moved from one state, which was hot to another state that was warm, and they were progressively getting colder.

Christ identified for them what they needed in order to restore themselves to true riches. They needed to receive a loan from Christ (the gold) which was his help in order to bridge the gulf or chasm that was beginning to exist between them and God. Christ was encouraging them to make use of him, so that they could be restored through him to their former standing.

Christ was the one that was tried in the fire. He went through severe testing and came out pure therefore, what he would give them, would have the same attributes. This was the only way for them to be rich according to God's standard.

The question that each of us must ask ourselves is, are we truly rich? Are we like the Laodicean church who put too much weight on material wealth and started to forsake true wealth, which resided in Christ alone? Where does your riches lie?

CRUCIFIXION CHALLENGE

As followers of Christ, we owe him the credit for both internal and external *riches*. It is through Christ that we are abundantly filled and blessed with good things.

MEDITATION

In Matthew 19:16-26, we are told of the rich young ruler. This young man had a heart for God. He desired to serve God, but he had an affection to material things. The fact is he loved his wealth more. What is interesting is that he would not have known it except that Christ put his finger directly on the issue. Jesus exposed his **Achilles heel**.

Often we are unaware of the obstacles, hindrances, ensnarement's, or entanglements that the enemy has in our lives. We are usually made aware of them only when God gives us an opportunity to see them. When was the last time you seized an opportunity from God to truly see the things that block your continued walk with Jesus? What did you do about it?

THE 21 DAY

Many things qualify as riches on earth such as the accumulation of property, having a large bank account, possessing fine degrees or titles, having many children, or having a phenomenal job that pays well. The lesson of the rich young ruler is that if our love for these things is stronger than our love for God then it is easier for a camel to go through the eye of a needle than for us to enter into the kingdom of heaven. Why?

The truth is that our riches would be a god unto us. It would be standing in the position that should be reserved for God alone.

The 15 MINUTE CHALLENGE

By the grace of God, take time today to lay your *riches* before him. Give *all* of them to him. Everything that is valuable to you should be entrusted to Christ. Once you have emptied all before Jesus, ask him to fill you with true riches. Ask him to help you to get hotter for him and to have the right focus in life. Seek him for the right

CRUCIFIXION CHALLENGE

perspective and for discernment concerning your children, job, finances, etc. Let him resurrect all that concerns you to the glory of God!

PRAYER

Father, we thank you that you are establishing your kingdom in us. We thank you that as we give all to you that you will fashion them as they ought to be.

Father, we do not know how to create, but we ask that you fill our mouths with words that will *create new life* in those that hear them. Help us to introduce *light* to those we meet. We bless your name for we know that as we submit to you all will be well with us.

Thank you Lord for your patient love. If there is anything that would separate us from you identify it for us in Jesus name. We know you will never leave us and we are asking you to help us to never leave you. We want to give you all of our love, all of our hearts,

THE 21 DAY

and all of our minds. Lord, help us for we do not know how to do it, but we desire to be taught, in Jesus name amen.

CHALLENGE

DAY 13

LOVE

SOPHIA

PRAYER

Lord, we thank you for making us rich though Christ Jesus! You have blessed us with proper *vision*. You have pointed out to us what is valuable in life.

Father, we entrust all that you have given us into your hands. We know that you are able to defend and keep. Lord, we ask you to preserve our lives and keep our souls. We ask that you help us to be alert and vigilant against the adversary. Ignite us with your *fire* so that we are ablaze for you. We refuse to be lukewarm. We refuse to grow colder. Father, help us to bring down the kingdom of the enemy wherever we encounter it in the name of Jesus, amen.

SCRIPTURAL FOCUS

"Saying with a loud voice, Worthy is the Lamb that was slain to receive power, and riches, and wisdom, and strength, and honour, and glory, and blessing."
⚜ Revelation 5:12

"Saying, amen: Blessing, and glory, and wisdom, and thanksgiving, and honour, and power, and might, be unto our God for ever and ever. amen."
⚜ Revelation 7:12

Thou art worthy, O Lord, to receive glory and honour and power: for thou hast created all things, and for thy pleasure they are and were created."
⚜ Revelation 4:11

Being in Christ Jesus means that we are lovers of *heat* and *light*. When we begin to get lukewarm or start to grow cold,

CRUCIFIXION CHALLENGE

it indicates that we have a problem. We are no longer tightly connected to the fire stream of God. When we walk in the natural sun, we get hot, our body temperature rises, and we begin to sweat. Likewise, when we walk with Christ the Light of the world we are to get hot. We are to be on fire for the things of God. Every so often, we should take time to take our temperature. Are we growing hotter or getting colder?

LESSON

Wisdom. What is wisdom?

The Hebrew word for **wisdom** is **Sophia**. It means to be broad and full of intelligence. It is to have knowledge in both divine and human things. It is having the ability to interpret dreams, the skills to manage affairs, and having farsightedness in our relationships with men who are not followers of Christ Jesus. It is knowing how to share the gospel of Christ with others, possessing the ability to form the best plans one can use, and using the best means for executing those plans.

Joseph is an example of one who operated with *wisdom*. He was placed over Potiphar's house (Genesis 39) and then placed over the domain of Pharaoh (land of Egypt, Genesis 41:41).

However, Christ is the ultimate example of *wisdom* at work, for he was and is a skilled manager. He was entrusted with the possessions of God the Father as the eldest Son. He is responsible for all of the property, wealth, and possessions of God. In 1 Corinthians 1:30 we are told,

"But of him are ye in Christ Jesus, who of God is made unto us wisdom, and righteousness, and sanctification, and redemption:"

CRUCIFIXION CHALLENGE

This verse clearly states who our *wisdom is*, and who the source of our *wisdom is*. Therefore, no believer should ever credit their abilities to any other source, but to Christ Jesus for to do so is to rob him or what is rightfully his.

MEDITATION

Whom do you credit for your wisdom? Have you ever taken the credit that belonged to God?

When we perceive something or we get a revelation about a matter, it is easy to take the credit for ourselves. To believe that is our innate ability. However, it is not. Christ pointed this out to Peter after he had correctly answered that Jesus was indeed the "Christ, the Son of the living God."

"And Jesus answered and said unto him, Blessed art thou, Simon Barjona: for flesh and blood hath not revealed it unto thee, but my Father which is in heaven."
⚜ Matthew 16:17

THE 21 DAY

The knowledge of both human and divine things originates with God for the believer. Therefore, we are to worship him as the originator of wisdom. When we do, we will be able to accomplish all that wisdom dictates us to do. In every situation, we will have the ability and skill to accomplish the purpose of God with confidence.

The 16 MINUTE CHALLENGE

Christ was made wisdom for us. As we walk with him, his nature will overwrite our former programing if we let it. However, at any point in the process we can opt out. If you desire to have wisdom rule in you and are determined to worship the Lord with your wisdom then invest 16 minutes to speak to him about it. Pour out your heart to him. Ask him to help shape you completely. Ask him to allow wisdom to fulfill its work in you.

CRUCIFIXION CHALLENGE

PRAYER

Father, we thank you for Jesus who is *wisdom* unto us. We bless you because you are such a good God. You have thought of all that we would need to complete our journey and you have provided it for us. Father, activate wisdom in us so we will know what to do, when to do it, and how to do what you desire as we live our lives on the earth. Father, help us to grow in faith. Help us to excel in confidence in you. Bless us to be courageous as we face new situations and challenges. Thank you for hearing us and answering us, in Jesus name, amen.

CHALLENGE DAY 14

THE VALUE

OF CHRIST

PRAYER

Father, we thank you for another day here on the land of the living. We thank you for protecting and keeping our families and us. Today help us to continue to grow in grace and wisdom to the *glory* of the Son and to the *honor* of the Father. Help us to live our lives in a way that will pour out on you all that is rightfully yours we pray in Jesus name, amen.

THE 21 DAY

SCRIPTURAL FOCUS

"Saying with a loud voice, Worthy is the Lamb that was slain to receive power, and riches, and wisdom, and strength, and honour, and glory, and blessing."
⚜ Revelation 5:12

"Saying, amen: Blessing, and glory, and wisdom, and thanksgiving, and honour, and power, and might, be unto our God for ever and ever. amen."
⚜ Revelation 7:12

Thou art worthy, O Lord, to receive glory and honour and power: for thou hast created all things, and for thy pleasure they are and were created."
⚜ Revelation 4:11

In our last lesson, we learned about *wisdom*. The *wisdom* that God provides is capable of addressing any and all situations that arises in life. It is a comprehensive *wisdom*. It enables us to be specialists in anything as the need arises. However, the *wisdom* of God is for those who are submitted to God, it is for those abiding in Christ

CRUCIFIXION CHALLENGE

Jesus, and who are willing to live lives of sacrificial *love*. It is a life prepared for the chosen few (Matthew 22:14).

LESSON

In this lesson we will focus on what **honor** is. To give honor is to value something because of its price or by fixing a value upon something. It is the charge paid or received for a person or thing bought or sold. It refers to a *business transaction* in which someone paid the penalty or suffered the punishment as compensation for someone or something.

When we give *honor* to Christ, it should be with the full understanding of the cost he paid for our *freedom*. It should be with the recognition of the suffering that he underwent for our release from bondage. When we give others *honor* in the place of Christ it is to despise what he has done for us. All that we need has been provided for us through Christ, our provisions, healing, mental health, safety, skill, revelation, knowledge, clothing, food, shelter etc. When we credit others with what God has provided through Jesus, we rob him of the *honor* due to him.

Christ is the first of all things therefore; he is to be first in line for *honor*.

MEDITATION

If you have ever watched an award ceremony then you probably have seen individuals who received a reward begin to list a host of people they would like to honor or give thanks. Occasionally a person may thank God. How often do you take the time to thank God? When you are acknowledged on your job, at your church, or in school do you think that you owe this honor to God? Do you give it to him publically?

When people are telling you how great you are or what a fantastic job you did, do you wonder if it could be a trap or trick of the enemy? Do you wonder if he is flattering you so that you will

CRUCIFIXION CHALLENGE

stumble and fall? Does it cross your mind that he is subtly wooing you to absorb the honor that belongs to God? Have you taken time to ask the Lord if the honor that you are receiving is the one that comes from him?

The 17 MINUTE CHALLENGE

Today invest 17 minutes to think about past honors. Did God honor you or was it a snare of the enemy? Did other blessings flow from the honor or did it precede a fall? Was the honor of your own making or one that was divinely inspired?

Ask the Lord to search your heart. Do you want to give Jesus sincere honor or do you want it for yourself? If you want to honor Christ, ask him to reveal to you the price he paid in a way that you will understand and remember *forever*. Ask him to sear it on your heart and engrave it on your mind, so that it will help you make wise choices, which will honor him.

THE 21 DAY

PRAYER

Lord, we thank you for the price that you paid for our *salvation*. We know that it cost you *everything* and you held back *nothing*. At times, it is hard to comprehend your type of love, but we desire to understand it and to live it. Lord, we want to honor you with all that we do. The choices that we make, the thoughts that we have, the words that we speak. Father, we want to wait on you to honor us before men. We do not want men to honor us for it is fleeting and it fades. However, when you honor us it is eternal and it changes not. Lord, we will wait upon you. Help us to become sons that are worthy of honor from you. Root us in truth, guide us with wisdom, and keep us in love we pray, amen.

CHALLENGE

DAY 15

JUDGE

GOD GOOD ALWAYS

PRAYER

Father, we thank you for another day in your presence. You are a great and awesome God. We are astounded by your love and faithfulness. We glorify and honor you because you have made yourself known to us. We realize the value of having a relationship with you. We acknowledge what you have saved us from and we say thank you.

Thank you for the opportunity to know, worship, and love you. Help us to grow in truth, to become brighter lights, so that we can become active voices for righteousness.

Father, help us not to lose the battle by remaining silent. In every area where we find the enemy stir us to speak out, "It is written, the Lord has said, or I rebuke you in the name of the Lord." Father, fill our mouths with a timely and appropriate response so that we can silence the enemy, put him to flight, frustrate his plans, free your people, set a watch around the camp, and usher in your kingdom we pray, amen.

SCRIPTURAL FOCUS

"Saying with a loud voice, Worthy is the Lamb that was slain to receive power, and riches, and wisdom, and strength, and honour, and glory, and blessing."
⚜ Revelation 5:12

"Saying, amen: Blessing, and glory, and wisdom, and thanksgiving, and honour, and power, and might, be unto our God for ever and ever. amen."
⚜ Revelation 7:12

CRUCIFIXION CHALLENGE

Thou art worthy, O Lord, to receive glory and honour and power: for thou hast created all things, and for thy pleasure they are and were created."
⚜ Revelation 4:11

Yesterday we learned about **honor**. What value you have placed on the worth of Christ in your life? Is he the pearl of great price for you? Will you sell all you have to obtain it?

"Again, the kingdom of heaven is like unto a merchant man, seeking goodly pearls: Who, when he had found one pearl of great price, went and sold all that he had, and bought it."
⚜ Matthew 13:45-46

God placed a high value on the lives of men for he spared nothing. He gave his most prized possession. He sent his son. The one who ruled the heavens with him. The one who created all that is seen. The one who manages the affairs of his Father, with honor, truth, light, holiness, and righteousness. He gave his first-born so that we could be born into the kingdom of light. What value do you place on your life? And how will that influence how you live from henceforth?

LESSON

Today's lesson will focus on the Greek word ***doxa***. Woven into this four-letter word for ***glory*** is a wealth of understanding. *Doxa* is to give an opinion, hold a view, or issue a judgment about a person and it is always in the *good*. It is to seem, be reputed as, or to be accounted. It is to think, to judge, or determine.

The ability to judge a matter correctly occurs when our eyes are exposed to evidence or proof of a thing. It is when we are shown or taught the truth of a matter.

The Bible reveals a few of the ways God ensures that the eyes of men are enlightened.

CRUCIFIXION CHALLENGE

"But the anointing which ye have received of him abideth in you, and ye need not that any man teach you: but as the same anointing teacheth you of all things, and is truth, and is no lie, and even as it hath taught you, ye shall abide in him."
⚜ 1 John 2:27

"For whosoever shall call upon the name of the Lord shall be saved. How then shall they call on him in whom they have not believed? and how shall they believe in him of whom they have not heard? and how shall they hear without a preacher? And how shall they preach, except they be sent? as it is written, How beautiful are the feet of them that preach the gospel of peace, and bring glad tidings of good things!"
⚜ Romans 14:13-15

"And he said, How can I, except some man should guide me? And he desired Philip that he would come up and sit with him."
⚜ Acts 8:31

THE 21 DAY

God works through the anointing, through preachers, and teachers in order to open the way of opportunity for those who are willing to conclude for themselves who he is. Individuals must settle for themselves what they believe or whether what is said about Christ is accurate. Does he possess the character or nature that is attributed to him?

At some point in time, we will be required to answer the same question that Christ posed to his disciples. "Whom say ye that I am?"

"And he saith unto them, But whom say ye that I am? And Peter answereth and saith unto him, Thou art the Christ."
⚜ Mark 8:29

Our answer to this question will establish whether we crown God and Jesus with the glory, they rightly deserve. When we think of Christ we are to think of him in good terms, our opinion of him should result in our giving him praise and honor. We are to recognize his brightness, splendor, magnificence, and preeminence. We are to have a good opinion of his majesty, grace, and excellence always.

Do we acknowledge the perfection of his deity? The gloriousness of his position, his character, or his work? Do our actions testify to the high regard that we have for him? Or do other things get the glory that is due to him and him alone?

"Therefore let no man glory in men. For all things are your's; Whether Paul, or Apollos, or Cephas, or the world, or life, or death, or things present, or things to come; all are your's; And ye are Christ's; and Christ is God's."
⚜ 1 Corinthians 3:21-23

MEDITATION

When we understand the full implications of the word *doxa*, we see that God has truly put forth a compelling case before the world. He has established his love for mankind even at the sacrifice of his son. As further evidence of love Jesus willingly went to the cross to lay down his life for his friends (John 15:13).

The issue of *glory* is established through how we respond to the evidence.

What have you concluded based on the evidence God has shown to you? Is there anyone else who is worthy of such glory? How will you establish your glory unto him? What is your opinion of him now that you have weighed the evidence?

In Romans 8:35-39, we get a glimpse of how Paul put to use evidence and drew a conclusion about the love of God. In like manner, we are to weigh all things and then come to a *sound conclusion*.

The 18 MINUTE CHALLENGE

There are times that we all have given others what rightly belongs to God whether by ignorance or by presumption. When we realize that, we have erred in judgment we can either make it right through repentance or ignore it. God will not overlook our robbery. He will take note of it. He will provide opportunities for us to turn, confess, and to repent. If we refuse, our actions will speak out against us, as will our inner witnesses.

"Jesus answered and said unto him, If a man love me, he will keep my words: and my Father will love him, and we will come unto him, and make our abode with him."
⚜ John 14:23

"Know ye not that ye are the temple of God, and that the Spirit of God dwelleth in you?"
⚜ 1 Corinthians 3:16

Invest 18 minutes today to sit quietly in the presence of God. Ask him to reveal any areas where you have given his *glory* to another. Are there areas where you drew the wrong conclusion based on the evidence? Did you judge a matter incorrectly?

Giving glory to God involves how we assess and judge things. Are we judging them the way that God would or does? Are we establishing his standard in our lives and in the lives of our children? Are we preferential to those we like and legalistic to those we do not? Do we establish God's words and teaching wherever we go? (Acts 10:34, Romans 2:11, Malachi 3:6, Numbers 23:19, 1 Corinthians 5).

Giving God the glory that is due to him is done on a daily basis. It is established in every situation. It is revealed by how we choose to live our lives. True glory is given to God as we walk the path of Christ. It is established as we utilize and apply what God has provided to help us overcome and be victorious in life.

PRAYER

Father, help us to establish your glory in all that we do. We do not want to rob you. We do not want to live in ways that dishonor or tarnish your reputation on the earth. Father, when men see us we desire that they see you. We want our words to be similar to

CRUCIFIXION CHALLENGE

that of Christ. (John 14:7-9, 2 Corinthians 3:2, 2 Samuel 12:14).

"Jesus saith unto him, Have I been so long time with you, and yet hast thou not known me, Philip? he that hath seen me hath seen the Father; and how sayest thou then, Shew us the Father?"
⚜ John 14:9

Help us oh Lord to achieve the standard that was set for us to follow. It is not by our strength, nor by our might, nor by our sheer willpower, but only by your spirit. Strengthen us. Enable us. Direct and keep us. Where our eyes are darkened, pierce them with *light*. Where our hearts are hardened please transplant them in Jesus name we pray, amen (Ezekiel 36:26).

CHALLENGE DAY 16

PUBLISHED

PRAISE

PRAYER

Lord, we thank you for open eyes. We thank you for the *light* of Christ that has pierced them. We ask that you help us to adjust to the *pure light* of God. It is our desire to exist in your *light.* We do not want to be shadow dwellers nor do we want to be like those groping in the dark. Help us not to revert to former times, but that we will leave the shame of those days behind us. Help us not to carry the yoke of former days into our future in the name of Jesus.

THE 21 DAY

Father, we love you not as you deserve. Help us to grow in our understanding so that our love for you will increase. That it will become deeper, truer, and purer in the name of Jesus we pray, amen.

SCRIPTURAL FOCUS

"Saying with a loud voice, Worthy is the Lamb that was slain to receive power, and riches, and wisdom, and strength, and honour, and glory, and blessing."
⚜ Revelation 5:12

"Saying, amen: Blessing, and glory, and wisdom, and thanksgiving, and honour, and power, and might, be unto our God for ever and ever. amen."
⚜ Revelation 7:12

Thou art worthy, O Lord, to receive glory and honour and power: for thou hast created all things, and for thy pleasure they are and were created."
⚜ Revelation 4:11

CRUCIFIXION CHALLENGE

LESSON

Today we will learn about **blessing**. *Eulogia* is the Greek word used for *blessing* in Revelation 5:12. Blessing is to give praise, to release a public speech, or to publish a text in praise of something or someone. It is to express with polished language or fine words the goodness of someone. To bless Christ is to be weighty in our sayings, teaching, discussions, thinking, meditations, considerations, and calculations. It is to point out with words the goodness of God and of Christ Jesus.

The meaning however, goes deeper than this, for it also means to be well, to act well, and to prosper. When we look at the beatitudes in Matthew 5:3-12, we see a pattern emerge. One that expresses the notion that these individuals are happy in spite of their circumstances. When we look at their situation through the lens of *blessing*, we realize that through the equipping of Christ, they were able to weather the storms of life. If we abide in Christ all will be well for us, we will prosper. In every situation, we will have the ability to act well.

When we do these blessings, await us. If we are poor in spirit, which means that we are reduced to being beggars, then the kingdom of heaven is ours. If we suffer greatly and are in deep mourning then Christ will come to our side, he will draw near to us to give us comfort, to exhort, teach, and encourage us.

MEDITATION

Do we mention Christ with weightiness of words? Do we affirm his goodness publicly or in writing? Do we speak of how he ministers in government and in creation? Do we speak highly of his wisdom and power? Do we tell others of his role in "life", morally, physically, socially, ethically, financially, and spiritually? Or do we give the *blessings*, which belong to Christ to others?

CRUCIFIXION CHALLENGE

The 19 MINUTE CHALLENGE

God is worthy of our *blessings*! Today invest 19 minutes in *blessing* God. Follow the lead of Holy Spirit. He will let you know if you are to sing praises, speak words to others, or write a message, which lavishes Jesus with *blessings*. Whatever he instructs you to do, do it with a *willing* heart. May the joy of the Lord fill you to overflowing as you embark on 19 minutes with the Lord.

PRAYER

Father, you know all that we go through. You are aware of the challenges we face, the pressures that are pressing in on all sides. Lord, there is nothing that we face that you have not foreseen. Lord, lead us as we go through the trials. Keep us focused and determined as we endure the fire. Father, help us to bless you in spite of the circumstances. Lord, in this battle help us to win.

THE 21 DAY

Fill our mouths with songs and our hearts with your peace. We will not be assimilated as one who does not know God. If we have spoken as one who is foolish forgive us and establish us a new in you this day we pray.

"But he said unto her, Thou speakest as one of the foolish women speaketh. What? shall we receive good at the hand of God, and shall we not receive evil? In all this did not Job sin with his lips."
⚜ Job 2:10

Spirit of wisdom we ask that you fill us to overflowing in Jesus name, amen (1 Corinthians 1:30).

CHALLENGE

DAY 17

GOD

CHOSE TO

PRAYER

Lord, it is wonderful to still be on the land of the living. It is so sweet to be full of expectations. Let today be a glorious day. Order our steps as you fill us with your presence. Put your words on our lips. Cause us to release life and hope wherever we go this day we pray, in Jesus name, amen.

THE 21 DAY

SCRIPTURAL FOCUS

"Saying with a loud voice, Worthy is the Lamb that was slain to receive power, and riches, and wisdom, and strength, and honour, and glory, and blessing."
⚜ Revelation 5:12

"Saying, amen: Blessing, and glory, and wisdom, and thanksgiving, and honour, and power, and might, be unto our God for ever and ever. amen."
⚜ Revelation 7:12

Thou art worthy, O Lord, to receive glory and honour and power: for thou hast created all things, and for thy pleasure they are and were created."
⚜ Revelation 4:11

We are on the 17th day of our challenge. It is a special day for it represents the union of spiritual order with ordinal order. (http://www.jesus.707.cz/E.W.Bullinger%20-Number%20in%20scripture.pdf)

CRUCIFIXION CHALLENGE

It represents the ordering of all God has revealed to us thus far in the challenge. As we apply the knowledge that we are obtaining we are being groomed in proper spiritual *understanding* and growing in divine *wisdom*. By now, we should be witnessing an element of spiritual order beginning to manifest in our lives and in our consciousness. An order that looks a little different from what was before. We should feel spiritually cleaner and healthier. If this is the case for you than you will want to release praises unto God! ***Eulogia! Eulogia! Eulogia!*** To the most high God, amen.

LESSON

The focus of today's lesson is Revelation 4:11, the last portion of the verse, which says, "... *and for thy pleasure they are and were created.*" Our primary focus will be on the word *pleasure*.

THE 21 DAY

The Greek word ***thelēma*** is used for the word ***pleasure***. It means to desire, choose, determine, or to wish. It is to will, intend, or to have in mind. However, it also means to take delight in. As we investigate the deeper meanings of the word, we discover it means to choose, prefer, to elect, or to take for oneself. *Thelēma* gets its primary meaning from the word ***airō***, which means to elevate, lift up, or to raise up. This indicates that it is God's desire to raise us up by his hand, to carry us away, to move us from where we were (the enemies kingdom) to where he is (the kingdom of life) and he does it by force.

God has taken us from among the dead and brought us into the presence of the living. He has made a way for us to cease living as dead men and live as spiritual men. Why did it please God to make a way for us? Why did he choose to lift us up? Why did he elect to save us?

CRUCIFIXION CHALLENGE

God chose from eternity past that he would incline himself to us in order to place us where he determined we were and are to sit. He knew all that we would do and he did not change his mind. The way was fraught with complications and setbacks yet he stayed the course. Why? Because he has determined what *shall* be. This is what he wants, what he wishes, what he desires to exist. God has decided that he will bless mankind and he has done so though Christ Jesus.

What is evident here is that whatever God determines to be comes into being. This is a fulfillment of his name and his nature. The name *Jehovah* (**Yĕhovah**) means the existing One. When we explore the root meaning of the word we learn it means to fall out, cause things to happen, to come to pass, but it also means to covet, wait longingly, wish, sigh, incline, desire, crave, lust after, and to long for.

God is patiently waiting on us to become like him. He is desirous for us to have his *full* nature. He wants us to crave for the things that are good, healthy and wise. He wants us to have lusts and desires that are rooted in righteousness and holiness. He wants to be the source from which all our wishes, wants, and desires stem. In essence, God wants us to fulfill the purpose for which we were created. We are to be a pleasure unto the Lord. The way to achieve that is to allow his nature to manifest completely within us without hindrance, without it being tarnished or diminished. The path to achieving this is to allow him to continually, lift us to higher realms of existence in him through Christ Jesus.

As children of God, we are called to exist in the higher rarer air or regions. We are not earth dwellers for we are citizens of the kingdom of heaven. When we embrace this reality we will be well on our way to obtaining the spiritual perfection that God intends for those he calls *sons*. The reality is that only true sons will be able to please God for they alone will believe *unwaveringly* in him.

CRUCIFIXION CHALLENGE

"But without faith it is impossible to please him: for he that cometh to God must believe that he is, and that he is a rewarder of them that diligently seek him."
⚜ *Hebrews 11:6*

MEDITATION

Where are you seated right now? Are you residing in heavenly realms or in earthly territories? Do you want to ascend to the high place of the Lord? What is fighting against you? Your emotions? Thoughts? Desires? Friends? Family?

Are there things standing in your way? Are you willing to remove them? Are you willing to silence all other voices except for that of the Savior?

THE 21 DAY

The 20 MINUTE CHALLENGE

http://www.jesus.707.cz/E.W.Bullinger%20-Number%20in%20scripture.pdf

The number 20 represents *expectancy*. What do you expect from God? What can God expect from you? Take 20 minutes in the presence of the Lord to explore this matter with him. List them. Meditate on them. Concentrate them to him.

PRAYER

Father, we lay before you our *expectations*. We expect to grow in the knowledge of Christ. We expect that our understanding will be enlightened. We expect to learn how to please you more with our lives.

Father, we expect to grow in love. We expect to be tested and refined to the glory of God. We expect to be filled with Holy Spirit and to be led into all truth by him. We expect that in the end, we will hear well done, and we will be allowed into your eternal place

CRUCIFIXION CHALLENGE

of rest. If there is anything that would prevent us from fulfilling these expectations, we ask that you help us dislodge it right now in the name of Jesus we pray, amen.

CHALLENGE

DAY 18

ABSOLUTELY

NOTHING

PRAYER

Father, we thank you for being a present help in the time of trouble. We thank you that when the enemy is active you are more active on the behalf of your children.

Father, we thank you that when the enemy springs his traps that you have devised a way of escape. Lord, we take comfort in knowing that all we face you have faced with victory. The temptations that befall us are those that are common to man but as we abide in you all will be well with us.

THE 21 DAY

Help us to be victorious in all things. Reveal secret things unto us. Open hidden doors for us. Help us to hear with spiritual ears and to see with spiritual eyes. Speak to us and ignite our faith. Reveal unto us so that we can walk the path that will led us on the straight course of life. Fill our hearts with *unadulterated* love for you. Let there be no seed of division within us. We want to cleave to you in all things, at all times, and in all seasons, in Jesus name amen.

SCRIPTURAL FOCUS

"Hereafter I will not talk much with you: for the prince of this world cometh, and hath nothing in me."
⚜ John 14:30

Yesterday we learned the reason that all things were created. It was not so God could feel good with himself. It was so he could take *delight* in lifting, aiding, and delivering us from the hands of the enemy. From before creation took place in the Garden of Eden God purposed what he wanted to transpire. God was determined to bless man by lifting earthen clay beings, created from the dirt under his feet to a place of esteem. He desired to seat us in heavenly realms alongside Christ Jesus. Although none of us are worthy of such an honor, God intended it for us from the beginning... praise God. For such a wonderful gift all that can be said is *thank you*. Let us live lives to honor God because of his determination to save us.

LESSON

What a profound statement Christ made when he declared that the prince of this world had *nothing* in him! What did he mean? What was the significance of his words?

The Greek word *oudeis* was used to explain the word *nothing*. It means no one and nothing. It is a definitive or absolute negative when one is expecting an affirmative answer. Satan had absolutely nothing, not even a little thing in Christ. From Jesus' statement, we know that Satan was unable to penetrate the armor of God, which clothed our savior (Ephesians 6:10-18).

"(For the weapons of our warfare are not carnal, but mighty through God to the pulling down of strong holds;)"
⚜ 2 Corinthians 10:4

We know that the armor that he wore enabled him to destroy the works of the enemy. It protected him as he went through tests, trials, and tribulation.

"He that committeth sin is of the devil; for the devil sinneth from the beginning. For this purpose the Son of God was manifested, that he might destroy the works of the devil."
⚜ 1 John 3:8

Jesus was made visible for the purpose of destruction. The word *manifest* means to make known by teaching, to be realized, to make what has been hidden or unknown known. Christ was made evident, apparent, and plainly recognizable for destroying the works of the enemy. When we allow Christ to

CRUCIFIXION CHALLENGE

be evident in our lives the works of the enemy will likewise be destroyed.

In a sense, God dispatched his best operative and equipped him with the best technology that was the armor of God, and sent him to complete a dangerous mission for the lives of countless men hung on his triumph. At least this is how it appears from our standpoint.

But was this truly the case? Was there ever a danger of Christ not fulfilling his mission? Or failing at his assignment? Christ was the seed of the Father himself. He was formed by righteousness, holiness, love, and light. His members were charged with every good virtue. The only way he could fall was if he yielded to temptation. If he chose to sin. In this respect, he was in the exact same situation as Adam.

Jesus was and is the Word of God. He came forth from the mouth of God. Every word that flows from the Word of the Father accomplishes its task for which it is sent. Therefore, as the living and manifested Word of the Father, Jesus **had to accomplish that which he was sent to do**. Not only would he complete the task, but he would prosper in it.

"In the beginning was the Word, and the Word was with God, and the Word was God."
⚜ John 1:1

"So shall my word be that goeth forth out of my mouth: it shall not return unto me void, but it shall accomplish that which I please, and it shall prosper in the thing whereto I sent it."
⚜ Isaiah 55:11

Likewise, if we apply the Word of God to every situation it will accomplish what it is ordained to do. When we speak the Word of God, it prospers in the thing where it is sent. When we use the protective gear that God himself used we are protected from the enemy and we will triumph over him and his kingdom.

CRUCIFIXION CHALLENGE

As we put to use all that God the Father has provided for us, we will begin to tear down the stronghold of the enemy. We will set him to flight. We will be transformed more into the likeness of Jesus and eventually we too will be able to declare that the enemy has nothing in us.

This is the mark of an overcomer. This is what true triumph looks like. A life that is obedient to God will *close all doors and access points to the enemy*. It gives him no point of entry, no place which he can commence an action. It does not allow him any opportunity to disrupt, interfere, or hinder anything. It does not give him the time to do anything for all is watched and carefully guarded. In the purest sense, the mark of an overcomer is to render the enemy unemployed in his life.

THE 21 DAY

MEDITATION

How active is the enemy in your life? Are you wearing the combat gear of God? Are you properly applying the Word of God? Do you *truly* believe the Word of God unwaveringly? Are you ready to battle for complete victory?

The 21 MINUTE CHALLENGE

Today spend 21 minutes with the Lord. For the first 7 minutes, confess where you have fallen short in your walk with the Lord. In the second 7 minutes, ask the Lord to help you to properly arm yourself daily. In the last 7 minutes, ask him to fill your mind and mouth with the words you need for this season to ensure *victory*.

The Word of God will never fail. It is an impossibility therefore, we can trust that what it is sent forth to do it will do. Christ is the Word of God therefore, if we believe that he will accomplish in us all that he was charged to do by the Father it **will be done.**

CRUCIFIXION CHALLENGE

PRAYER

Father, thank you that there is nothing that is impossible for you. Thank you for making a way for us to be overcomers in the earth and in heavenly realms. Lord, we bless you. We thank you that as we apply all that you have given to us it will separate us from the enemy and separate the enemy from us. We want to make him unemployed, in Jesus name. We want him to be useless. Father, we cast down the shame that the enemy has tried to cover us in. Let him wear his own shame, in the name of Jesus.

Father, help us to honor you with our obedience as Jesus did. Cause us to walk in robes of brighter glory. Help us to move from faith to faith. Lord, we know that with your Word over our lives we will accomplish all that we are supposed to do to the glory and honor of your name, amen.

CHALLENGE DAY 19

CALLED

TO BE A NIKAO

PRAYER

Father, we thank you for your goodness toward us. We bless you for you are an *awesome* God. Our hearts long for when we can declare that the enemy has *nothing* in us. Keep us on the path that will assure our brightness in Jesus. Provide opportunities that will lead us into *greater light*. Give us openings to lead others into the brilliance of your presence we pray in Jesus name, amen.

THE 21 DAY

SCRIPTURAL FOCUS

"These things I have spoken unto you, that in me ye might have peace. In the world ye shall have tribulation: but be of good cheer; I have overcome the world."
⚜ John 16:33

"For whatsoever is born of God overcometh the world: and this is the victory that overcometh the world, even our faith."
⚜ 1 John 5:4

"And they overcame him by the blood of the Lamb, and by the word of their testimony; and they loved not their lives unto the death."
⚜ Revelation 12:11

Yesterday we learned that the enemy had nothing in Christ Jesus. What is remarkable is that it is God's goal that the enemy have nothing in us as well. However, this is impossible for us to achieve without Christ. It is only through Jesus that we can evict the enemy wherever we find him. As we allow Christ to manifest in our lives,

CRUCIFIXION CHALLENGE

the destruction of the enemy's works will take place. Therefore, it is the enemy's objective to prevent us from manifesting Christ in our lives fully for this will allow him to exercise influence and power over our members, which are not fully subjected to Christ. Now is the time for us to decide to follow Christ *all the way*.

LESSON

Today's study will focus on the words *overcometh*, *overcome*, and *overcame*. The Greek word *nikaō* was used for all three words. *Nikaō* means to conquer, to come off victorious, and to carry away the victory. It is when one goes to court to be arraigned or to win one's case. It is to maintain one's cause. It is to subdue, conquer, or prevail over someone or something in order to get the *victory*.

Overcoming is demonstrated when one holds fast to faith even unto death against the power of the foe.

THE 21 DAY

When we examine the Thayer's Greek Lexicon, we discover that *overcoming* involves causing an enemy to repent of the wrong he has done to you by using the force of *goodness* or *kindness*. It is to keep oneself *spotless* from the strategies of the enemy and to remain unharmed. It involves *freeing oneself* from the power of the enemy.

As believers, our testimonies facilitate our ability to overcome. Christ has made a way for victory; however, we must use the force of his goodness to establish or bring it in. In a sense, we live our lives in front of a heavenly court. Every action, word, thought, or deed is recorded. They either maintain or uphold the case of Christ or they do not. When we uphold the case of Christ, we are in reality prevailing by the blood of Jesus through the application of *divine goodness*. The objective is to rid ourselves of the shame of the enemy. To allow him to wear his own shame.

CRUCIFIXION CHALLENGE

His enemies will I clothe with shame: but upon himself shall his crown flourish."
⚜ Psalm 132:18

Let mine adversaries be clothed with shame, and let them cover themselves with their own confusion, as with a mantle."
⚜ Psalm 109:29

People who were bought by the blood of Christ have a duty to testify laid upon them. The testimony is how they bear witness to God daily through the way they live their lives. The standard of God is that we are to be spotless therefore; we cannot allow the enemy to have anything in us. We cannot turn a blind eye. We cannot tolerate within ourselves anything, which does not originate in the *goodness of God*.

THE 21 DAY

Although the devil will try to deceive us into thinking, God will accept a small vice or a tiny sin it is a lie. God's standard is unwavering. He said we are to be spotless, without wrinkle, and without blemish. In order to be victorious we must embrace what it means to be overcomers in God's eyes. It is for us to be like him *pure light*.

MEDITATION

What cause are you trying to maintain? Is it your individuality? Your way or the cause of Christ? Whenever the enemy starts his work or your flesh begins to speak and act out do, you render a judgment that upholds the standard of God? Do you try to subdue your flesh? Do you exercise dominion over the enemy? What do you do to ensure *victory* as God defines it?

CRUCIFIXION CHALLENGE

The 22 MINUTE CHALLENGE

Spend 22 minutes in the presence of the Lord. Ask Holy Spirit to open your mind and bring back to your remembrance any occurrences where you have not upheld the cause of Christ. It is time for you to go into court and take the stand before God. Give your testimony. Judge the matter as God judges it. Call sin what it is. Judge the works of the enemy as unholy, unrighteous, wrong, wicked, and sinful. Make the enemy wear his own shame. Declare your desire and intent. How will you secure victory from now on? What do you intend to do in order to live the life of an overcomer?

PRAYER

Father, the enemy is guilty of dishonoring you. He is guilty of tarnishing your creation. He is guilty of leading masses of your people down the path of destruction. Lord, it is our earnest desire that you will rescue those whom you have called by name. Open their eyes and deliver them from the hands of the enemy. Father, for those of us who have allowed the enemy to work in our members please help us to subdue him in the name of Jesus.

As we take steps today to evict him, we ask that you close the door unto him. We want to be spotless, without blemish, and without wrinkle. We throw off every yoke of bondage including confusion, fear, anger, strife, bitterness, wounding, unquenchable grief, depression, and any other tool or vehicle that the enemy has used or is trying to use influence our lives or to hold us hostage, in the name of Jesus.

Lord, we bless you for you have paved the way for our victory. You have opened unto us the overcomer's path unto us. Help us to use the force of your *goodness* to establish victory wherever we go to the shame of the enemy and to the glory of God we pray, amen.

CHALLENGE

DAY 20

FOUNDATION

OF KINGS

PRAYER

Father, thank you that you have made a way for us to be overcomers. We are so thankful that Jesus overcame the world. And because he has, we know that the way has been made for us to do the same. Father, be with us as you were with him. Keep us as you kept him. Enlighten and teach us as you enlightened and taught him. Father, we ask that you would even pour out on us an extra measure of *faith* so that we will remain firm in truth, that we would be unwavering in the name of Jesus. The storms of life get turbulent and rough but we ask that you release peace unto us so that no matter what we face we will be at rest in the safety of your presence, amen.

SCRIPTURAL FOCUS

"And hath made us kings and priests unto God and his Father; to him be glory and dominion for ever and ever. amen."
⚜ Revelation 1:6

"And hast made us unto our God kings and priests: and we shall reign on the earth."
⚜ Revelation 5:10

"A Psalm of David. The LORD said unto my Lord, Sit thou at my right hand, until I make thine enemies thy footstool."
⚜ Psalms 110:1

"Which in his times he shall shew, who is the blessed and only Potentate, the King of kings, and Lord of lords;"
⚜ 1 Timothy 6:15

CRUCIFIXION CHALLENGE

"And he hath on his vesture and on his thigh a name written, KING OF KINGS, AND LORD OF LORDS."
⚜ Revelation 19:16

Last time we learned what it means to be a *Nikaō*. Overcomers' are those who uphold the case of Christ. They testify against the work of the enemy and establish what is true in every situation. They do not allow the enemy to bear false witness against God. If God has said it then it is so and the matter is established. It is our aim to be overcomers in all. **We are to cause the enemy to wear his own shame. We are to declare him guilty with our words, actions, deeds, and motives. The enemy is to be unemployed in the lives of overcomers.** May this be our end through the work of Christ in our lives, amen.

THE 21 DAY

LESSON

What is it to be a *king*? A *king* is one who leads people. He is a commander, the lord of the land, and he is a prince. A *king* is one who has a foundation of power. The Greek meaning for the word ***king* (*basileus*)** is walking, the foot, a stepping, or that with which one-steps. Therefore, a king is denoted by the way in which he walks or steps through life on the foundation of power. As believers, how we walk on the foundation of Christ will indicate whether we are kings or not.

Christ is referred to as the **King of Kings.** He is the first of all that God has determined to come into existence. He is the beginning of all that was created for God's pleasure (Colossians 1:15). Therefore, he is the beginning of the walk of every king. It is through the work of Christ that we have been made kings. It was not so that we could lord over people or so that we could have our own way. It was so the pleasure of God could and would be fulfilled in the earth.

CRUCIFIXION CHALLENGE

All that God intended was and is under the supervision of the Son. God has full confidence in Christ's ability to govern his possessions for Christ is the Word of God which when sent forth it accomplishes all that the Father intends it to do. The Word does not question the speaker. The Word does not deviate from the purpose for which it has been sent. The Word is obedient and focused. It pierces through until it achieves the goal or intent of God. In like manner as kings in training, we are to allow the Word of God to accomplish the purpose of God in our lives. The Word is to fashion, teach, guide, and protect us. The Word of God will *deliver* us and *enable* us to be *triumphant* over the works of the enemy.

If we allow the Spirit of Christ to have his way, we will be established on the firm foundation of the power of God. Our walk will be sound. Our footing sure and our rule amazing to the glory of God. It is only by allowing the work, which was begun in us to be completed that we will be eternally established as kings. It is at the completion of this process that we will know that we are indeed kings after the likeness of the *King of kings*.

Before we can rule over others, we need to be able to govern ourselves. We need to apply the Word of God to our lives so that our walk and footing will be sound. It is time to take the beam out of our own eyes. It is time for us to live lives of truthfulness and sincerity.

"Thou hypocrite, first cast out the beam out of thine own eye; and then shalt thou see clearly to cast out the mote out of thy brother's eye."
⚜ Matthew 7:5

We may not know or comprehend the areas in which we have fallen short of the glory of God, but if we seek him, he will reveal it to us. If we inquire of him, he will not allow it to remain a mystery unto us. It is God's desire that the enemy be weeded out of our lives and being. It is his desire that we operate as kings after the likeness of Christ therefore; he will not ignore us

CRUCIFIXION CHALLENGE

if we seek to gain spiritual insight. He will not turn a deaf ear if we cry out for wisdom and understanding.

In ages past, many kings ruled over God's people however, few were good, most were bad. Today God is giving us an opportunity to decide whether we want to be a temporal king or an eternal king. Do we want to rule in earthly realms or in heavenly quarters? God has called you to be a *basileus* after the likeness of Jesus. Are you willing to go through the whole process? Allow the foundation of power, which resides in Christ to be established in you.

MEDITATION

What kind of king are you currently? What are the things that can hinder your being a king after the likeness of Christ? Are you willing to get rid of those things? What things in your life do you need help with so that you will rule to the glory of God?

THE 21 DAY

The 23 MINUTE CHALLENGE

Many times, we go before God and we do all the talking. We pour out our wants, desires, needs, yearnings, etc. We do not always stay in his presence long enough to hear his response to our requests. Today invest 23 minutes just sitting in the presence of God. Attend to him. Listen to him. Cry out, "Father, I am seeking to hear from you today. I am silently waiting. I need to know what you have to say about my life. About my walk. About my kingship."

PRAYER

Father, we thank you that Jesus is the *King of kings*. We desire to walk in the path that you have laid out for us. Father, our foundation is your power and our example is your Son. Enable us to grow, learn, and to succeed in Jesus name. We declare Jesus King over us. Our lives are subject to the *King of kings*, amen.

CHALLENGE

DAY 21

ANOINTED FOR

DISTINCTION

PRAYER

Lord, we thank you that you are establishing our steps so we do not stumble or fall. We bless you that our feet are planted on the solid foundation of your Word. What a privilege you have given us. Help us to value it. To treasure it. To savor it in the name of Jesus. Let us not take it for granted.

Father, we speak to our feet they are clothed in peace and they *will* carry the gospel of Christ. They will take us in the paths of righteousness. They will go where you lead. They will not fail us nor will they become weak or tired, in Jesus name.

SCRIPTURAL FOCUS

"And hath made us kings and priests unto God and his Father; to him be glory and dominion for ever and ever. amen."
⚜ Revelation 1:6

"And hast made us unto our God kings and priests: and we shall reign on the earth."
⚜ Revelation 5:10

"A Psalm of David. The LORD said unto my Lord, Sit thou at my right hand, until I make thine enemies thy footstool."
⚜ Psalms 110:1

"Which in his times he shall shew, who is the blessed and only Potentate, the King of kings, and Lord of lords;"
⚜ 1 Timothy 6:15

CRUCIFIXION CHALLENGE

"And he hath on his vesture and on his thigh a name written, KING OF KINGS, AND LORD OF LORDS."
⚜ Revelation 19:16

What a wonderful thing it is to be a *king* in training! In order to be a king after the likeness of Christ we have to be able to follow orders. The mark of **obedience** must rest on us. Christ was *obedient* to God unto the cross (Philippians 2:8, 1Corinthians 15:27-28). In like manner, we are to be *obedient* to Christ unto the cross. We are to die daily to sin (1 Corinthians 15:31).

We are called to righteousness. Righteousness cannot be established on a foundation of sin therefore, as *kings*, we are to rule our members with an iron rod (Psalm 2:9). It is time to break the enemy in pieces, shattering the evidence of darkness like earthenware.

"Ask of me, and I shall give thee the heathen for thine inheritance, and the uttermost parts of the earth for thy

possession. Thou shalt break them with a rod of iron; thou shalt dash them in pieces like a potter's vessel. Be wise now therefore, O ye kings: be instructed, ye judges of the earth. Serve the Lord with fear, and rejoice with trembling."
⚜ Psalm 2:8-11

It is time that we possess all of our being. If we ask, God will enable us to regain all. No longer will the enemy have the ability to take us captive at his will, but rather we will break his works to the glory of God (2 Timothy 2:26).

LESSON

Today we will focus on the Greek word **kyrios** that means **lord**. Woven into its meaning is the understanding of supremacy. It denotes ownership, one who is the possessor or disposer of a thing. It is one who has control. A *lord* is a master, chief, or sovereign of a state. *Kyrios* is a title of honor that communicates abundant respect and reverence, but it is also refers to how a servant greets his master. The main thing about *kyrios* is the way in which it honors a man of distinction.

To be distinguished is to be different. It is a contrast between similar people or things. It is similar to how God distinguished light from darkness (Genesis 1:4). It is also, what God did in Exodus 8:23, where he demonstrated the difference between his people who lived in Goshen and those who did not.

In Malachi 3:18, once again God spoke of distinction between the righteous and the wicked between those who served him and those who did not.

What is evident is that God distinguishes his possessions from other things or people. The Levites and priests were separated from among the other tribes to serve the Lord as were the articles used in service to God (1 Chronicles 28:13). Therefore, as believers we should expect God to distinguish us from other people who inhabit the earth. In fact, we should desire it for it is God's way of honoring us among men.

THE 21 DAY

The honor that God bestows on us is not one that we can create or fashion for ourselves. Nor is it an honor that men place upon us! It is a spiritual mark of approval that comes with the anointing of God. The anointing enables us to grow in righteousness. It helps us to make the line of distinction more evident in how we live our lives on the earth. As *lords* under Jesus, our first duty is to take possession of ourselves because we are lords in training. We are to govern ourselves according to the standards of God. Therefore, we are to be possessors of the things God has made available to us and dispose of what he has not given unto us. One of our prime assets is love. We are to cultivate this, hold on to it, and disseminate it (John 15:12).

"A new commandment I give unto you, That ye love one another; as I have loved you, that ye also love one another. By this shall all men know that ye are my disciples, if ye have love one to another."
⚜ John 13:34-35

CRUCIFIXION CHALLENGE

In fact, it is the only debt that cannot be paid off. We may be able to finish paying off our mortgages or a student loans, but the debt of love will continue for it has no expiration date and the amount owed is eternal.

"Owe no man any thing, but to love one another: for he that loveth another hath fulfilled the law."
⚜ Romans 13:8

As lords, we are to possess the fruits of the spirit. It is by our fruit that others will know that we are lords of Christ (Matthew 7:16).

"But the fruit of the Spirit is love, joy, peace, longsuffering, gentleness, goodness, faith, Meekness, temperance: against such there is no law."
⚜ Galatians 5:22-23

The establishment of the fruit of God is contingent on our possession of a sound mind. We have to allow the mind of Christ to be in us. Once the process has begun, it is imperative that we hold firm to the mind of Christ

THE 21 DAY

refusing to allow our old mind to supersede the lordship of Christ in us.

"Let this mind be in you, which was also in Christ Jesus:"
✢ Philippians 2:5

It is only with the right mind that we can discern the value of the fruits of God. It is only the mind of Christ that blesses us with the wisdom needed to know how, when, or if to address a matter. It is the mind of the Savior that enables us to know when we are not walking or operating in love.

Furthermore, as *lords* of Christ we are called to be disposers. With the authority that Christ has given us, we are able to fight against principalities, rulers of darkness, spiritual wickedness, and powers (Luke 10:19, Ephesians 6:12-18). Our first duty is to apply the delegated authority of Jesus to ourselves. We are to weed out the enemy from among our members. We are to ruthlessly pluck out the beam from our own eyes (Matthew 7:5). If a part of our being causes us to sin, we

CRUCIFIXION CHALLENGE

are to amputate it (Matthew 5:30). We are to take whatever steps are necessary to ensure our survival in the way of God regardless of the cost or the level of pain involved.

As *lords*, we must be willing to dispose of what is dear to us even though it will wound or maim us. It is this determination that will testify to the great reverence and respect we have for the Lord. Anything less will not allow us to be counted among the *lords of Christ* for it will show that we love ourselves more than we love him.

"Nevertheless the foundation of God standeth sure, having this seal, The Lord knoweth them that are his. And, let every one that nameth the name of Christ depart from iniquity. But in a great house there are not only vessels of gold and of silver, but also of wood and of earth; and some to honour, and some to dishonour."
✝ 2 Timothy 2:19-20

THE 21 DAY

MEDITATION

The mark of a lord is one who departs from iniquity. A lord knows what to hold on to and what to dispose of. God has given us time to soberly reflect on which type of vessel we desire to be one of honor or one of dishonor.

Are you willing to pluck out your eye? Or to go through life maimed? These things are not necessarily physical, but could be spiritual, emotional, or mental. Are we willing to love Christ more than our children or spouse? Are we willing to allow a wayward child to go their course and trust God to deal with them? Or will we be like Eli turning a blind eye?

Are we willing to trust God for our finances and maintain our joy in the Lord or will we allow the enemy to drive us crazy thorough worry and fretting? Will we allow the devil to introduce his solutions rather than opting to wait on God?

CRUCIFIXION CHALLENGE

The 24 MINUTE CHALLENGE

Spend 24 minutes in the presence of God. Ask him to identify the areas that you need to focus on in order to continue your training as a *lord*. Ask him for the grace to pluck and cut. Ask him to help you to believe him above all else. If in the past the line of distinction in your life was not as prominent as it should have been, ask him to make it visible to all including yourself, in the name of Jesus.

PRAYER

Father, I thank you that you have called us to be *lords* in training. Establish us in your ways. Help us to honor you with our hearts, minds, and actions. Let them be unified under the banner of Christ. If there is any contradiction in us we are to eradicate them. Help us to dispose of what needs to be disposed of. Give us the wisdom needed so that we can be fruitful and prosperous, in the name of Jesus amen.

CONCLUSION

Congratulations, you have successfully completed day 21 of the CRUCIFIXION CHALLENGE!

It is my earnest hope that you were *truly* blessed by the challenge. The path of death is a hard one to travel; however, it is not an impossible one.

God has established the reality of **victory** for us through Christ Jesus. If we are *faithful* and remain steeped in *belief* then there is nothing impossible for us to achieve.

The survival of nations rests on our shoulders. As we shine the light of Christ brightly many will be drawn to him, nations will be saved, and the lost will be found.

As we die to our old nature, we weaken Satan's hold on our lives but also his

THE 21 DAY

hold on the earth. Our death diminishes his influence, it retards his growth, and it pushes back his kingdom, as it advances the kingdom of God.

This battle will be won *only* if we follow the leading of God and the example of Christ completely.

Be blessed! May strength and the peace of God be yours, in Jesus name, amen.

"The LORD bless thee, and keep thee: The LORD make his face shine upon thee, and be gracious unto thee: The LORD lift up his countenance upon thee, and give thee peace."

⚜ Numbers 6:24-26

CRUCIFIXION CHALLENGE